©Copyright, 2016

By

Jamera Napier & Art Blackburn, Sr.

ISBN: 978-0-692-42959-4

Cover designed by Jamera Napier & Art Blackburn, Sr.

Cover layout Sally Rice

DG PUBLISHING PRESS
Tallahassee, Florida 32304
www.dgpublishingpress.com

Table of Contents

Introduction

Are you a stepparent? Are you feeling like you are gift to an existing family? Well you are! That is correct. You have been chosen by the paternal or maternal parent to first, be their partner in life, therefore, you have ultimately been chosen to step up, where the other parent has stepped out, stepped down, or stepped back, in order raise one of the greatest assets to a family, the children. No your role is not to replace the past but to embrace the future.

Did you know that when a stepchild pulls up to your table that they are bringing a whole army that is invisible to you and maybe parts of the army has become invisible to the stepchild. Your naked eye and mind's eye only see the child. However, if you had the hindsight and foresight to see behind the child, its behavior whether it be good or bad, and then you might see the invisible marching army. This army has been perfecting its skills behind your back and right underneath your nose then sent to you. Like a Trojan horse sitting in enemy camp waiting on you to go to sleep so they can attack.

Stepparents are gift to an existing family. Now – you may not see it nor believe it considering the actions of the stepchildren, the co-parent and that invisible army of other people, emotions, society, lack of understanding, lack of laws of protections, lack of appreciation, lack of recognition, lack of not knowing what to do or what to expect next but we are hopeful that after reading this book that you, the paternal or maternal parent of your stepchildren and the invisible army will see you as the great gift you are and recognize that you have been chosen.

Step Parenting: Don't change the title – Change the game!

This book's primary objectives are to provide some personal insights to help you or someone you know successfully survive step parenting. The information shared will be based on real experiences and methods of how these real experiences lead to a realistic way of surviving and succeeding at step parenting.

This book will in no way be inclusive of all of the scenarios that can or might be applicable to our diverse lives as we enter and/or exit step parenting. Step parenting is exclusive in the fact that it is one of few positions that does not discriminate or exclude any one class of people, sex, generation, race, color, creed, sexual orientation, religion, political party, profession, social class, financial disposition, education levels, and forgotten past or infinite future. It is all encompassing.

Some of these incidents in this synopsis may read to be unbelievable and some may be so real you may think we are talking about your current situations. The people or incidents you may discover as you relive these experiences shared between these pages are real, happened to very real people and yes - you may duplicate the good things shared but do not forget the not-so-good things. Why? Because some of the not-so-good situations turned into good situations which may assist you or someone you may know who is a stepparent or they are on the road to becoming a stepparent.

In between these pages, we will answer the questions:

- How to look for warning signs when danger is approaching you as a stepparent
- How to survive the X-Factor (drama from the X {mother or father of the children})
- How to help your partner (The custodial parent of the children) Step UP!
- How to help your stepchildren fit into your lives and not you around their lives
- How to demonstrate ways of communicating for you and your new blended family
- How to regain control in a situation that is not supported by the law
- How to change and remove the cloud of negativity associated with step parenting to a shower of praise for step parenting
- How to identify people with whom to share your step parenting concerns and those people with whom to share your experience with reservation.
- How to demand survival of your blended family and avoid the circumstances that created the need for a blended family.

 Hindsight 20-20 will be used in this book to help you have the foresight not to fall for the camouflaged deceptions. Look for the dark sunglasses and the caption **[Art's 20-20 Hindsight:]** (Art is the co-author and biological father to my stepchildren).

In the Christian belief, there is a recount of the story about Jesus, the Son of God, which speaks to His immaculate conception to His mother Mary and His stepfather Joseph. Jesus was not from the seed of the man called Joseph in the Bible; however, Joseph was the husband to Mary and the given father of Jesus.

How did our culture miss this big opportunity for blended families to be recognized by this century's bestselling book (The Bible)? To be more like Jesus is what we teach and what we strive for if you are a believer in Christianity. Was it just an oversight or a blatant way of hiding the truth of the destiny of families and possibly a good way to be successful at blending families?

If this one concealed fact was taught or shared, maybe today stepparents would have some rights to protect them, rights to have a say of their chosen children; maybe biological parents would recognize the gift that their children have just been awarded the benefit of having not two parents that are not together by choice or default but possibly four parents, and less drama would be tolerated from the adults or the children due to boundaries put in place to support the newly blended families.

We will go into more detail about this biblical story inside of this book; however, in summary – Would it not be perfect ...IF stepchildren could be more like Jesus, stepparents could be more like Joseph and this is really [1]BIG If the X-Factor, custodial parent or the birth parent could be more like God, the Father. (He is a God that could do the impossible but He chose to assist and not insist). He did not need Joseph or anyone else.

What I am saying?

Ok - Here it is: The parents of the children are separated or divorced by choice or demand. One of the parents has made the conscience decision to move forward into a new loving relationship. He or she has made the best decision to seek happiness in their lives after their last relationship.

We think the X Factor parent should comply with the following suggestions:

1. Be a *supportive* X and not a *destructive* X.
2. Be an *invisible* X when the children are not in your custody.
3. Be an *invisible* X in the new relationship.
4. Be an *encouraging* and *informative* X
5. Be a part of the team and help transition your children *positively*.
6. Be *a motivator*: move forward and stop tripping *backwards*.
7. Be a *positive* "X" and not a *negative* "X"
8. Be a *carpenter*: Build yourself up, the children and your "X" (husband or wife).
9. Be an *obedient servant* of the law: Be *divorced*!

---

[1] BIG Acronym" Because I am GOD" originated concept & business name: Mr. Tony White

10. Be *brave*. Support your child's stepmom or stepdad (They have to step into the shoes of parenting your child when they are with the natural parent).
11. Be a single parent with children or give up the child support and the children.
12. Learn to let your family ride on the camel and you walk away.
13. Be responsible – accept the fate you helped decide and do not try to duplicate the failure ... Plan to be successful.
14. Be a Pioneer. Do not fall for the statistically okeydokey (failures).
15. Be a good hater - Duplicate the good and dismiss your bad.
16. Stop hating, baiting, faking and stating, "It is about the children."
17. Stop hurting and start helping ensure the best for the children, yourself and their natural and stepparent.
18. The X Factor parent should not be intrusive, abusive or manipulative indirectly through the children or directly in any form or fashion into their X's new blended family.

About the title of this book: Lethal Weapon

This book's main title is a piggy back off of the title of a late 80's movie series titled Lethal Weapon starring Mel Gibson and Danny Glover. These shows were about a veteran cop Murtaugh, who is partnered with a young suicidal cop, Riggs. Both had one thing in common – preferring to work alone. Now they must learn to work with one another to stop crime. Working together for a common goal paved the way for them to go from complete strangers to welcoming each other as family.

The co-author and I recognized that we, standing together sometimes side by side and at other times one in front of the other, are a *Lethal Weapon*. Unlike the fictional characters (Murtaugh and Riggs) in the movie, we had the blessing of choosing each other to be partners in our relationship. We willingly joined hearts and minds to stand together and fight for our love, our family, our relationship, our respect and his children (now my stepchildren). We had to learn to work with one another to stop the hidden dangers of the destruction from his ex-wife, society, our children, the law and the silence of acceptable abuse to divorced and single parents with children and stepparents.

We are convinced that a blended family can be happy and successful but not without some careful observations, due diligence, understandings and actions.

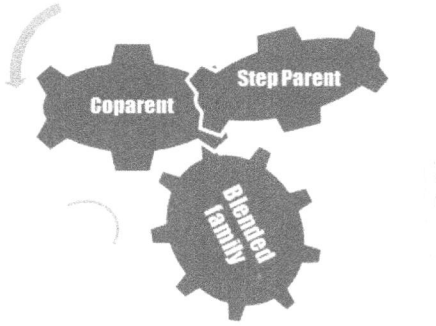

A Method to the Madness

"A method to the madness" is a phrase that was first used in the play titled "Hamlet" by Shakespeare. It has taken a familiar account in conversations when confusion is in the midst of trying to be understood. According to Dictionary.com the phrase is defined often as a plan behind a person's apparently inexplicable (unexplainable) behavior.

Step parenting is not a new process, but it is lacking the newness of its rapid development in today's and yesterday's world. Step parenting is not given the crown that it truly deserves based on stories being told, fairy tales and, of course, those of stepparents and custodial parents that have not successfully met the challenge of step parenting.

I am a proud stepparent. I did not become a gratified stepparent overnight, and it was not an easy journey—not even close for me or the custodial parent of my stepchildren. Step parenting initially for me was like trying to see through the eyes of a blind man in a strange and unfamiliar place.

To allow truth to speak for itself, my becoming a stepparent was a journey that I will not care to repeat unless, of course, I have a road map of what to expect, how to handle the X factor and the stepchildren, emotions associated with step parenting and a custodial parent that was aware of his rights, boundaries and he was enlightened on the dynamics of blending his previous family with me. For example, a book titled <u>Take the "Step" Out of Step Parenting</u> would have made a great roadmap. If "step" was taken away from step parenting then that would leave just "parenting." It is just mathematical!

[Word equation: Step Parenting – Step = Parenting]

In other words – if you have the words 'step parenting' and you take away the word 'step' only the word 'parenting' is left.

FACT 01: Surviving step parenting successfully will be a PROCESS!

What is a process? A process as defined by Webster online dictionary is a series of actions or steps taken in order to achieve a particular end. In the process of processing, you will have peaks and valleys in each stage.

In relative terms, you will have to take steps forward, steps backward, steps around and side steps in order to be a successful stepparent. These steps you are taking could be fun if you had someone calling out the steps for you like when you are dancing "the cupid shuffle," "the hustle" or "line dancing," and all you have to do is just follow the leader's voiced commands. The joy or the fun of group dancing is learning the steps or at least trying to learn the steps while everyone around is doing the same steps to the music. This is not quite the case in the steps taken to successfully transition your life from your existing family to ultimately becoming a blended family.

In our human lives, there are four stages (steps) of birth, and each of these stages will happen, but they will not be identical for every person that experiences or witnesses them. They are unique to each individual just as step parenting is unique in everyone's case. The stages of our human existence are listed for introduction to some and review for others. Our lives begin with stages – processes and yes, these stages are repetitive until the end of life.

1. *Dilation (Early Labor, Active Labor, and Transition to second stage)*
2. *Baby moves through the birth canal (Begins with complete dilation and ends with the birth of the baby*
3. *After Birth (Pushing out of the placenta)*
4. *Recovery (Baby is Born)*

Let me introduce myself (co-author), I am Art, the biological parent. If I could shout these words from this book, I would say to each of you reading this text that "this step parenting business is a clueless mystery to which no one has a perfected plan or established directions to be successful".

In other words, life's experiences, stories heard or told, or even your fantasies will not come close to the reality of some of the hidden agendas, bad behaviors, rude responses, games played, sacrifices taken, tight lipped responses and the ignorance you will experience during the process of becoming a blended family. I am a pretty quiet type of guy so "no screaming;" however, we are hopeful that after reading this book, you will be in better control of your situations.

"It is better to take control than to be controlled" jrn

 **[Art's 20-20 Hindsight: Blindness]**

If I could have taken off my blinder and very dark sunglasses in the early years after my divorce, I would have done a lot of things differently. I would have tried to see everything in a different light, and I certainly would not have had a "do whatever it takes to keep the peace" attitude in my responses or actions.

I would be able to accept the idea that my X had an agenda and planned to use it as a tool of war against my happiness, my relationships (family and social), my finances, and my children. I would be able to see how my children were being directly and indirectly used as pawns (a person or entity used to further the purposes of another) in this same agenda. Yes, some of the agenda was intentional and some was just plain unacceptable X Factor behavior.

Like most divorced rookies, I was determined to be a good and responsible father which my X had a clear understanding of and used this knowledge to her advantage, none of which was truly to benefit the kids but only to overburden me in order to crowd out any woman from having a happy and fulfilling relationship with me and keep me from moving forward in the desired life I wanted for me and my children.

Jay, my chosen mate and stepmom of my children, attempted to help me to see the agenda, but I did not see the bright neon lights she was trying to show me. Remember, I said I was wearing very dark sunglasses and I have to admit they were blinders—I was blind like the late Ray Charles, the musician—blind! I had to come to grip with myself, my perception of divorce expectations, and X Factor behavior. It didn't really become clear until I internalized the fact that my X wanted me back, and she didn't want anyone to interfere with anything she wanted me to do especially with or for the children.

Here are some reasons why my X wanted me back or at least, under her control and maybe why yours wants you back in his or her life:

- Chores
- Handling the things that she didn't want to do
- Things that you can provide
- Your type of care/conversion
- Babysitting/her-his freedom
- Finances and resources

This may not be your case, but do not rule it out so fast. This very thought allowed me to revisit her past behavior and connect the behavior to a reason. It was at this point which was some years later unfortunately, I began to have a little insight into what to expect and to see if her behavior was a result of her agenda.

I tolerated my X's bad behavior in the past because I was used to her behavior. I just either ignored it or went around it. Maybe this was my easy way out and just trying to move ahead, and so I just expected and accepted it or ignored it altogether. Get this point – by my actions or lack of, I expected Jay to do the same. After all, I wanted to be a major part of my children's daily lives.

Well, at that time, it may have been okay, but when I think back and I consider the respect I deserved and the appearance of the lack of respect that may been left in the minds of Jay and my children, I should have refuted this behavior.

Some of the decisions I made not to take a stand for me and my chosen family were not the best decisions, and these responses did not go over well with Jay. Why should anyone coming into my life have to accept the bad behavior that I tolerated simply because I did?

I was so busy trying to walk in my future, still standing rigid in my past, that I almost lost my future for a past I did not want. It is my hope that you will not seek to judge my behavior but to monitor your behavior as you read and learn from my mistakes. That's correct—I will take one for the team in honor of making successful drama-free blended families.

I was in a mental turmoil of trying to keep peace with my X just because she had been granted custody of our children. I did not want our old relationship, and I was hoping that we both could be adults about the decisions made and move on positively with no emotional strings attached. I wanted custody of our children; the courts and society would not grant my wish. The law gave both us regulations, and I, of course, abided and she did not.

Fear, avoidance and my heartfelt desires had me gripped in quicksand that if I did not comply with her, she would do as she threatened: keep my children away from me, drag me back to court and/or continue to make sure happiness was not something I would have any time without her approval.

Jay, my children's stepmom, was a lifesaver for me and my children. She saw the good man than I am, the good father I desired to be and the X Factor's intentions. It was as if she had some type of magnifying glass with a crystal ball. She assisted me in realizing that my desire to be happy, a good father and respected should be a reality, not just a dream.

Today, I am the proud husband to a loving wife and a successful stepmom that has granted me my number 1 and number 2 desires: (1) To be loved, respected and appreciated simply for being me and (2) to assist me in showing my children how to love and be loved, and she receives all of the love I have to share.]

You will be able to be a successful stepparent or be with your chosen stepparent with success. Follow our lead to the path carved out of our method through the madness of taking the steps out of step parenting. Allow yourselves the opportunity to be happy with a stepparent or happy being a stepparent.

[20-20: End]

Judging

First things should always be first; take counting for example. If you were asked to count to 10 and you started counting 1, 2, 3, 4, 5, 6, 7, 8, 9, 10, some would agree that you successfully counted to ten but others like myself would disagree. Why? One to ten as shown above is the correct sequence but it is incomplete.

The number line starts with the number "0" then "1" follows the zero. You might think the zero has no value … well, until you consider the placement of the zero. Zero is primarily overlooked and misjudged because it is thought to have no value or significance.

If a zero follows a number then it adds value. Look at this number 1 and the number 2 as in the number 12. Now if you add a zero in the place behind the 1 and 2, you will get the number 120. So you see the zero is important and it does add value. You do recognize that 120 is greater than 12? This must be taken into consideration first even if you do not think the zero has any value. Our point here is to express when you are dealing with your X factor, society, and birth children consider everything as significant. Do not allow your thinking to decide oh "that act or word" means nothing its value is zero because now you are aware zero does have value.

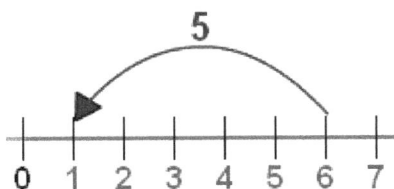

We challenge you to be objective and hold your judgment of me and the co-author until you have completed the reading, grasp our understanding and you have experienced firsthand the overwhelming challenges of being a stepparent and a biological parent trying to rebuild his or her pre-existing family into a well-adjusted blended family.

Have no fear. Help is on the way! So you ask, "What is judging?"

A judge is a public official appointed to hear and decide cases in a court of law. (The Judge's ruling should be based on the law of the land that has been set). He or she is assigned the job of making assessment.

To judge is to form an opinion or conclusion. Well, now! How do you form an opinion? Great question. To form an opinion is by thoroughly and carefully weighing of evidence and testing of the premise.

There are very few limiting laws set for step parenting so if you do decide to judge, what is the basis on which you will judge? What makes those standards which you select to judge incorrect or correct for the stepparent?

We welcome you to test and discern but do not condemn. Why? Because you don't know the heart, history, hope, hurt, help, the struggle, the success, the blindness, the underhandedness, the unseen, the seen or the sacrifices that I or my copartner (the coauthor) had to endure just to be able to say we are a success at being a good blended family.

Pictured above is a homemade green smoothie.

A smoothie is a creamy beverage made of fresh fruits and raw vegetables blended with juice, milk, and yogurt. It looked and tasted great in the end.

The beginning of this smoothie started with 12 different ingredients including raw vegetables that I would never imagine eating together, but once they were put together in a magic bullet blender and blended together, every shape, color, and taste changed from its original state to the desired state. Years prior, I would have prejudged a smoothie just because of its contents and never tried it.

A great tasting beverage full of essential vitamins, minerals and nutrients was produced. The fruits and vegetables were blended so well that I could not individually taste all of the ingredients: celery, carrots, banana, ginger, pineapple juice, 1% milk, cinnamon, apple, Greek yogurt, green peppers, kale and spinach.

Blending a family can be a smooth transition, once you get all of the right ingredients, the right tools, apply them and keep your goal in sight.

"It may not be easy to blend a family but a family can successfully be blended" jrn

Metamorphosis

Which came first?

One of my first elementary observations of a process of change was presented to me by mother. She is a beautiful spirited lady, a great mother to my siblings and me. She purchased an incubator, introduced it to my twin sister and me, and gave us two eggs to put in the incubator to show us how a chick could be born under the heat and other conditions without its mom. We had the responsibility of watching, turning the eggs until day 18, double checking the temperature and humidity, keeping the incubator closed and shying away from opening to see if there were any changes. The incubator had a clear dome window. We were little inquisitive girls at the time.

We excitedly agreed to do this experiment. She was always providing us with fun challenges. These challenges always prompted many questions and a lot of "I do not know what to expect" to my mother. She was very patient; she answered the questions to the best of her knowledge which was vast and then she would refer us to reference books to seek answers to the questions. She was the school librarian at this point in our lives.

I will add this note: we did not have the convenience of the internet when I say we had researched our answers. It was hand-to-book research. It physically was just that—going to a shelf and removing a volume from a set of hardback encyclopedias (for those of you who have no idea what an encyclopedia is it is a book or set of books giving information on many subjects or on many aspects of one subject and typically arranged alphabetically). NO GOOGLE at your fingertips and no spell check.

One day, approximately 21 days later—at the time I recall it seemed like an entire summer—the chicks were hatching in the incubator. I am not sure why my mother thought to do this experiment with my twin sister and me, but it has come to my mind as a great analogy to compare the stages of development of this step parenting business. Finally, the egg became a chick and we thought the hard part was over. No, we learned that the work had just begun. We did not know it then, but we had just become stepparents. The egg had been separated from its natural development to a simulated development and we were its surrogates.

My twin sister and I wanted a pet chick, and we were willing to do the steps instructed to make it happen, of course, with some impatience and curiosity. We were so excited about the chicks being born, but we had no idea that we would have to take care of the chicks after they were born. After a couple of days of feeding, cleaning, and monitoring the chicks, we wanted to give them away. It required too much of our time, and the novelty lost its luster very quickly. Taking care of them took much more time than we were desiring to give. We immaturely judged our responsibilities of what we believed to be our goal which was to see the chicks hatch but we were a little short sighted.

Maybe you had similar experience in learning about stages, for example:

- Not being able to stay at home without supervision
- No cooking until you reached a certain age
- Playing within eye sight of your parents or guardian
- Bed time
- Chores
- Dating
- Driving
- Spending the night away from home
- After school or before school attendance events
- Wearing makeup.

I shared that view into my childhood to demonstrate that for me, stages were a standard. Learning about stages from my parents was definitely influential in my development from a child to adult, but it was also influential in my steps up and steps down the ladder of my growth from a single lady never married without children to step parenting.

If you have not experienced a perplexing moment of the "I don't know what to do next to make this family work" or "I don't understand why this is so difficult," then you will. One of the smartest things I learned during my learning stages of taking the "step" out of step parenting was "I do not have to have all the answers." I just need to ask the questions?

Stages are not a new concept in our lives and neither is step parenting. However, stages and step parenting can be like a brand new pair of shoes when the responsibility has become yours to assume willingly or by default.

New Shoes

Have you ever had the misfortune of finding the perfect pair of new shoes and they hurt your feet after wearing them? OMG! Shoes that you chose or they may have been chosen for you! You tried the shoes on for size, the style is so "you" then upon wearing them or sometimes no sooner than when you get them home, they do not fit so perfect. Shoe pain is right up there with a tooth ache pain. UGH!

The beauty of a new pair of shoes that hurt your feet is that you have some options that can be exercised to alleviate the discomfort from returning them to the store, trashing, exchanging, suffering, or never wearing them again. Several of these options may cross your mind as you take steps in your journey as a stepparent and that is REAL but the reality of this situation is not that simple. ☹

Blended families will, and I repeat, will have issues (pains) that must be dealt with great consideration and cannot be ignored.

FACT 02: Parenting is no easy job for the most part so when you kick it up a notch to a blended family, the word **NO** is important and **EASY** is absent from the equations.

In this book, we are going to Keep it Real (KIR-acronym that we borrowed from our brother Richard's vernacular). Do not and I repeat do not fool yourself into believing that television shows like the Brady Bunch (if you remember this sitcom of a blended family), where a lady had three daughters and a man had three sons and they married. They all shared the same household and had blending family issues which were all handled without disruptions of everyday life. The mom and dad, at least in the shows I watched, never were caught in the cross fires of blending.

OH yeah! Money was not an issue in this show either. Just so you are aware before we start unveiling issues, money is an issue for most blended families from the not so rich to the rich and famous. Remember that show was on television with a happy ending in each show ... actors, actresses, scripts, directors, props, extras and paychecks.

The truth is this step parenting is one ugly business from the beginning, but it can have a happy ending. Yes, after years, years (that word *years* was meant to be typed twice; it is not a typo) of development. We can say today our blended family, that is, dad, the two children, and I, the stepmom, have morphed into a butterfly of a relationship that started deep in larva stages.

From the beginning we will define stepparent. It has been brought to our attention that it is very important to understand the meaning of a word before you can become the word. We shall introduce some scenarios and the divine solutions that were employed, share some of the battles, successes, tools for step parenting, suggestions of teaching improvements, and close with the limitations of stepparents' legal rights—there are not any rights for stepparents automatically.

According to the English definition, "stepparent" refers to the man or woman who is married to someone's mother or father but who is not their (birth) real father or mother.

Stepparent defined by English Law Dictionary

> The spouse of a parent, who becomes the stepparent of that parent's children upon marriage. Stepparents are not legal parents of their spouse's children unless they complete a stepparent adoption, which requires the consent of the other legal parent or the termination of that parent's rights.

This definition has to be given a wider scope because of the change in the dynamics of the traditional family, marriage, divorce and co-habituating adults. We are not sure how to change dictionary.com, but we would like for you to keep an open mind as it relates to today's blended families.

Now that we got the definition out of the way, let's speak to how you may become or became stepparent.

A person can become a stepparent by legal definition and by today's family by the dating, cohabitating, and or marrying someone that has been divorced or separated from maternal mother or father with children.

So whether you legally assume the role or it was forced upon you, step parenting is one of the most difficult roles any adult will ever assume. See the chart below.

YOU	• No Children Never Married • Yes Children , Divorced
YOU Him or Her	• Yes Children Never Married • No Children Never Married
Him or Her	• Yes Children Never Married

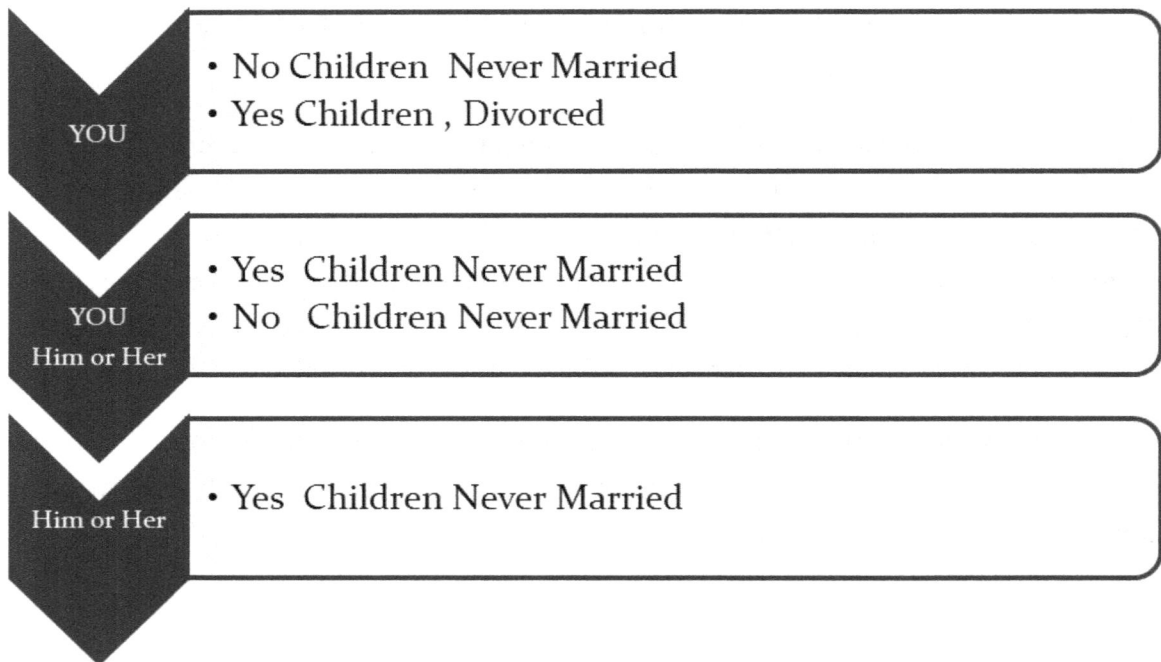

[Art's 20-20 Hindsight: Preferences]

It was not my desire to date a woman with no children or to date one with children. My desires were to meet, love, and marry a woman that could receive all the love I possessed in my own uniqueness then allow our loving relationship to be the guide for my children's development.

I had no preference, however, I did take into consideration, if she had children this would put me in the role of a stepparent most of the time and a parent to my children. I assumed that if I met a woman and she had children, they were awarded to her. This may not be the case for all but it is majority.

Our blended family is Jay- who had no children, my two children, and me. After initially getting to know Jay more intimately, I considered her to a better mother to my children than their maternal mother. She was naturally compassionate, maternal and supportive of both me and my children. She is very positive. You may know the type of person that always see the "good" before the "not so good". She chose to love my children simply because she had so much love for me.

I considered myself to be a good father and I would not have minded being the father of more children. I recognized early in the game of mother hood with my X that she was not very maternal. I did not wish to have any more children with her. I was more involved in the daily care of our children than she was. I am a man and I still have a lot of good-fun-loving nature in me, and I believe that children should be allowed to be children while they are children. So playing, laughing, hugging, coddling and, of course, some discipline were welcomed.

It was to my delight when I met Jay that she had a lot of energy and intelligence, and she did not meet a woman, man or child that did not take to her liking immediately. I thought to myself, "She will be a good match for me and my children."

The X was no longer part of this equation at least in my mind. I only regarded her as the mother of my children and nothing more.

[20-20: End]

So why become a stepparent? The reasons for becoming a stepparent are too many to list, but for keeping it real's (KIR) sake, we will list a few common ones:

1. Love
2. Dedication
3. Empathy
4. Sympathy
    a. Selfish Gain—Security of a spouse
    b. Parent for children
5. Default(Infidelity)
6. Default(Package Deal)
7. Default(The responsible thing to do)

However, you came into this role of step parenting, it is a job that will require work on your part, and you will have a chance to discover areas of opportunity to grow in areas you did not know even existed between you and your significant other, you and your stepchildren, you and your own birth children (if you have been blessed to birth), and you and the other parent(s) if they are alive.

If the other biological parent is deceased, it will be easier to fight ghosts of memories than the live biological parent. Becoming a stepparent of stepchildren may be a rewarding experience and a delight to your already great life; however, we must share these facts with you:

FACT 03:   YOU have no legal rights to these children unless the children are adopted by you. We have included legal rights documentation for your review. As of this date of publication, the law is as stated. Please check with your state of residence for your rights and responsibilities awarded and not awarded to you as a stepparent.

FACT 04:   Also be advised the X of your significant other may be aware of this lack of law and attempt to use it against you and your new relationship. Understand that FACT 3 is not a stumbling block in your decision to become a stepparent; nor should it prevent you from being a successful stepparent.

This is a very important discussion that should take place between you and your new spouse or cohabitating partner.

The awareness that the stepparents do not have any legal rights to the children basically means you as a stepparent have no legal say about the children's school, health, and major decisions. However, you will walk in the important shoes from co-parenting to providing financial support.

My stepdaughter was often informing me that I was not her mom in the absence of her father. On several occasions when she would share this update with me, I pondered whether this child needed medication. I was very much aware of this fact: I knew I did not birth her or any other children for that matter. One day, she informed me that I was not her mother and I was given the directions from our divine God how to respond. I asked her to join me in front of a mirror. I asked her if I looked anything like her or her mother. She responded, "No."

I said, "Good, I am glad you see that. I already knew it" I asked what was her name, her mom's name, then I asked her what was my name. She answered each question with the correct name. I said, "Then you are correct. I am not your mother. In case you did not know, I am your stepmother because your father and I chose each other."

I then informed her that she could remain in front of the mirror until she was sure whose daughter she was and whose stepdaughter she was. Then I told her, once she was sure about it, come to me to complete the task I asked her to complete. I mentioned that there may be a quiz to ensure we are both on the same page.

This is good news to learn. "Why?" you ask. Because when you are told these words and you will hear them, "You are not my mother or father," you will be able to respond correctly. For example, "That is true. Tell me something I do not already know" or "No, I am not your parent. I am your stepparent and glad about it."

This fact, if it is understood, can become a stepping stone for you, the stepchildren and your custodial parent by CATAPULTING all of you into the best and next levels of your relationships.

Imagine being in a classroom and you are a student in that classroom. It was not often that you had the right answer but on this particular day, the teacher asked the class a question and you knew the answer. You raised your hand, shook your arm to get the attention of all the standard know-it-alls, and then it happened. The teacher chose you. That is right. You were chosen and you got the chance to really shine and say the correct answer. It is a good feeling to be chosen!

_____

"To be chosen is better than not being chosen" Jrn

_____

The History of Step Parenting

How old is step parenting? How many years ago did someone actually take on the responsibility of loving and raising a non-biological child as their own child? There are at least two accounts of step parenting in the bible. We will begin with the account located in the New Testament.

For some of you, the facts that we are about to share may not have been revealed in this fashion. For some of you, it may take you a moment to consider these facts before agreeing with our perspective.

The story is recorded about 2000 years ago. It is the story about a man who is engaged to a virgin lady that has been gifted with a child from God. The father and the chosen daddy was not the same! The mother was carrying a child that did not belong to her fiancé. Now that sounds a bit confusing, but it is a true account. Let's break down this introduction into sentences.

I. Man engaged to virgin woman
II. Man marries woman that is gifted with child from God
III. Man becomes the first Stepparent in the new testament
IV. The child or the baby is the first STEP CHILD

This account can be found in the Bible in the book of Matthew and in the appendix of this book. The man is called Joseph, the woman is called Mary, and the baby is called **Jesus.** Jesus is the stepchild of the *chosen* man and the son of the *chosen* woman.

Take a moment to allow yourself time to wrap your mind around the previous text. Yes, if you look at it from where I am sitting, this is a fact. This conclusion is based on the definition of *stepparent* and how children become stepchildren.

Wow! Jesus a stepchild? Joseph is a stepdad! Can you see the illumination of the concept? It is true that stepparents are chosen. Stepparents are chosen!

The definition of *chosen* is to be elected or to be preferred. Mmm, this reason alone is enough for the X-factors to have a challenge accepting you as the stepparent to their children. You are chosen for the future and not frozen in the past.

FACT 05: The children should not have a choice in your mate. This is not a misprint. Jesus did not choose Joseph or Mary. His Father (God) did the selecting. Just KIR (Keeping it real)

Joseph did not plan the chain of events. It was not by his design to marry a woman that was all ready with child nor was it in Mary's plan to conceive a child prior to her marriage to Joseph. She did not plan to come to Joseph with a ready-made family; however, this is the way things turned out.

"If the plan is not divine, it is by design" Jamira Napier Lanh

How does it relate to you and your current situation? First, if you did not plan to become a stepparent by sabotaging a marriage or relationship, ensuring that the man or lady of your interest received custody of the children from their current relationship, at least part of the time and then you and the newly divided family becomes your dream come true; then it was not planned.

If you did not plan on making a baby and being without its mother or father whether it was by death or ending of relationship, then it was not the plan!

This story in the bible will not be identical to your life's story, but the end result is you are a custodial parent with children desiring to blend a family, you are single with no children desiring to blend a family, or you are a mom or dad with children seeking the blending of a mom or dad.

According to the Bible, Joseph, the stepfather was an honorable man that was a skilled carpenter, builder, and craftsman who was engaged to the Virgin Mary. He was a mortal human man – not a GOD.

We assume he was aware of how babies came into existence. He was an older man. He knew he had not touched his prized lady, and he was aware of the consequences of a woman in a compromised situation.

Jesus's stepfather was chosen, and GOD knew exactly what he was doing when he chose Joseph, the honorable Man. You can see that he was honorable by the foundation of the steps he chose to take to win or overcome this situation. Any lesser of a man may have taken a different approach or actions.

In the illustrations in the Bible, initially, Joseph wanted to take action. His emotions were enraged. He wanted to put Mary away by quietly divorcing her but he did not want Mary to be a public example. (Honorable).

Joseph was bothered to the point of his sleep being disturbed and in his dreams, an angel came to him and gave him the 411 or the inside story of what was really happening in his relationship. Imagine Joseph - the man, he was an older man about to be married to this young woman who had not known any man. He was to be her first and she was to be his bride. The wedding is not far away and he learns from her that she is with child and she was not touched by any human man. The lifestyles were not as forgiving about unwed mothers as we are today - her destiny was to be stoned to death. (TRUST)

Now, I believe in the Holy Bible and everything between its covers but I will not type these words and tell you if my husband or man came to me and told me, "Listen up, I know we are in this singular relationship, you know - just you and me … in the sheets. I know we agreed to this and only this type of relationship but then you see, this lady says she is carrying my child and I was told it was true in my dreams." "Really now" would only be the beginning of words that may leave my lips. Nah, she could have even posted it on FACEBOOK and I would not have trusted nor dared to believe it. (Not as honorable)

Honor and trust are two of the last characteristics of my character that would have been revealed in that fictional situation. Trust a dream! That is what Joseph of the Bible did … he trusted a dream. Maybe WWJD should stand for "What Would Joseph Do?" I'm just saying this Joseph and the Joseph discussed in Dream Takers both stood some tests of time and their dreams influenced their decisions.

In Joseph's case, he did as he was instructed; then he took on the responsibilities of "husband" to Mary and "stepfather" to JESUS. This honorable self-sacrificing man fled to Egypt with his blended family.

My mother, Madear as we passionately called her, would always say, "The children or that child did not ask to come to this earth, nor did it choose its parents; so the children have to be reared not steered."

Joseph's stepchild was from God – a blessing. The difference in our cases is stepchildren are 50% of the person whom you have been selected or chosen, a blessing, and 50% of someone else (in some case something else if you have to try to understand their behavior). Now this could be a case of big Messing.

Pin this to interest - the first stepparent in the new testament of the bible, if we look closely at the story, may have given steps to follow that may prove to be successful for you, the stepparent and you, the seeking biological parent.

Let's examine closely the steps taken by the first stepparent in the New Testament, Joseph.

- He was honest about his feeling.
- He was honorable.
- He trusted.
- He obeyed.
- He committed.
- He accepted.
- He showed self-sacrifice.
- He fled.
- He kept a tight lip about his situation.
- He acted in normality.
- He waited (demonstrated patience).
- He followed the law.
- He made the best of the changes.
- He supported.
- He provided.
- He protected.
- He taught.
- He listened.
- He loved.

Joseph was a descendant of royalty which implied that he had money. He had skills, was a pillar in the community, and people recognized him and paid attention to his life. The people did ask if Jesus was the carpenter's son (That is – paying attention or at least recognizing the family). Have you ever had the experience of being referenced first as your parents' child i.e., aren't one of Hazel and Paul's children? *Yes, one of the twins.*

The stepparent Joseph's entire life took on a change. He left the city for purpose and he may have been able to come back. He could have just closed up his house and shop long enough to serve the purpose and return. But he did not return. He and his blended family stayed away; he accepted the change of location and hid his family to protect and nourish his stepchild.

Ponder on these questions? Can you imagine the embarrassment, the sly comments, the passing conversations and the looks Joseph may have had to withstand from the people—his neighbors and friends? What he may have considered in his thoughts about Mary?

Can you imagine how Mary must have felt when Joseph told her that he would marry her in her compromising position and save her from gossip, ridicule and possibly death? Now just consider how you as a stepparent will be able to assist in the growth, development, transition of your new chosen mates children.

Stepparents back then and still today do not receive the honor or recognition that is deserving of some stepparents. How many books, movies, poems, or lyrics have you seen or read about successful stepparents or how many stepparents have received Stepparent-of-the-Year awards? Oh, I do not think that award exists. Stay tuned for Lethal Weapon II, the successful stepparent stories book. If you have a story you would like to share, please share it with us via the publisher or email: takingthestepoutlw@gmail.com and be a part of making the world take note of the greatness of good stepparents.

In the chapter entitled, *Ways to Show Appreciation for your Stepparent*, we would like to suggest some ways you can make your stepparent feel like he or she is worthy of a gold medal, the winners of the Super Bowl or King/Queen of Your Life.

I am convinced when both teams go to the Super Bowl, they both are aware that when the last play has been played that there will be one winner and one loser of the big game. The team that wins, without a doubt, is the winner of the Super Bowl.

Do you think the other team that made it to the Super Bowl is a loser? I don't! They may have lost the BIG game but they won all the other games just to get to the BIG game.

When is number 2 number 1? When you can see that you are the first in line behind number 1 if you are number 2. (It is all in the word *one* vs. the word *first*)

[Art's 20-20 Hindsight: Personal Conviction]

When I was young, my parents had gotten divorced. Even as a child, I recall it was an unpleasant experience filled with lots of negative emotions both felt and observed. Life got rough at times before and after the divorce. I personally noticed that the divorce not only separates the husband and wife but it also separates the extended family.

Remembering at how it was when my parents divorced, I made a vow to myself to do whatever it took to keep someone happy if it was within my power and to never get a divorce. I would exhaust every avenue before considering **divorce**. I could not let myself fall victim to divorce. I looked at some of the reasons why couples separated and made sure they were not in my path or behavior.

Well, I exhausted every option to stay in my marriage. Then I realized that I was not happy, and my children and I would suffer if I remained selfish to my conviction. I had this plan and I thought my X was on the same page. No divorce! I will stay in this for my kids' sake. Now, I am divorced by my choice. I am happier.

My kids had to make some adjustments, but kids have adjustments even when parents are not divorced. When I was married to my ex-wife, we had to move from our home state to another state for better employment opportunities. We had to recognize that in order to make a better life for ourselves and our kids, we had to relocate. Relocating took us away from our network of known existence, and our kids had to make the adjustment also.

With that said, divorce brought on its own adjustments. It was okay with my X when we were married to make adjustments, but she was not as flexible after the divorce, at least when it came to me. She wanted me to continue in the roles I played when it was convenient for her or it made convenience for the kids. Initially, I tried to make as little change as possible for the kids. They all stayed in the house, same schools, same church, and I moved into an apartment, changed social networks and tried to stay as close to the neighborhood as I could so that I could remain active in my kids daily lives.

No big change here for them—that was my goal. My X and I divorced, and we did not get our kids' input on our grownup decision to get a divorce. This was good for a while until I began to show interest in another relationship and in myself. I felt that I deserved more, for me and my children.

I adjusted to my personal vow to be happy and reaffirmed my vow to make Jay happy. Jay helped me to realize that as much as I was trying to keep things the same, a big change had happened. I was divorced and I was not going to the home of my children nightly. I had to understand and accept that with change, changing would be required.

[20-20: End]

Dreamtakers

Dreamtaker is a compound word that has not found its way into Webster's or any other dictionary so we will define it. That's correct, if there is not definition and we use the word, it is fair that we make a definition so there will be no misunderstanding of the term and how it will be used in our book.

Dreamtaker(s) is one who takes a dream away via misunderstanding, misinterpreting or sabotaging the dream.

There is a story in the Bible about this young boy who had several dreams, and he shared them with his brothers and his father. That was an okay thing to do – "share his dream with his family." When you think about it, Why NOT share your dreams with the people closest to you?

They were the people that should have his best interest. Do you agree that family and friends should have your best interest and maybe be your best cheerleader?

The young boy in this story was named Joseph, and God had given him a dream that he shared. By sharing it, it brought him several years of hardship by the hands of his brothers.

This story is a great parallel for stepparents. We will show you our interpretation of how it will demonstrate the importance of sharing your dreams, experiences, dislikes and frustrations with people that have no understanding, practical experience or appreciation for the role you must play as a stepparent.

In this story, after Joseph told his brothers about the dream, the very first thing they did was question him in a condescending way; then they went and told their father about the dream. The father then rebuked Joseph. Allow me to give you a little background into this story. Joseph was the baby boy of Jacob. Jacob had two wives and several sons and daughters. The Bible tells us that Joseph was favored mostly by his father because he was born unto him at a late age in life. I can imagine it is kind of like your parents allowing your children which are their grandchildren to get away with things and acts that would have cost you your teeth from the same adults. Back to the background of this story. Now because Joseph's brothers recognized that their father favored the baby Joseph more than them, they grew to hate Joseph. The hate grew to a higher level after Joseph shared his dream with them. I thought why would they be jealous? There was more than enough love to go around - they had been blessed with a mom and a stepmom, sisters, stepbrothers and stepsisters.

The dream basically implied that he would one day be ruler of them. Let's be real, who really wants someone that they do not like informing them that he will be ruler of them. Probably not the best step to take to get into your good grace. At age 17, Joseph was sent to check on his brothers who had traveled away from home for work. When he found his brothers, they had plotted against him, then put him in a dry well, and sold him to travelers. They camouflaged his absence to their father; then falsely supported their father in his mourning.

This story revealed to us that his brothers' jealousy of him caused them to act in ways that are not natural for brothers to act toward one another. Dreamtakers may do or have you doing one or more of the following:

1.   They may sell you out
2.   Have you wandering (lost)
3.   Seeking the advice of strangers
4.   Listening to hearsay
5.   Dreamtakers can always see a dreamer coming and begin to plot to kill your dream and you have no idea that you have been spotted
6.   Dreamtakers will remove your covering to assist in their plot to cover your absence in the presence of others
7.   Dreamtakers will not openly tell you they are a dream taker

To clarify it for you, if you share your stepparent experiences with someone who is not a stepparent, not planning on being a stepparent, has no positive experiences to relate to as a stepparent, and have never walked more than a weekend in your shoes or read this book, he or she may be a DREAMTAKER!

You will be allowing them, the Dreamtakers, to be in a position to misunderstand your frustrations, sabotage your dreams or your triumphs, which ever may be the case.

Sure you have known this person for a life time and he or she is a great friend, great parent or even a great associate but lacks the experience of being a stepparent and may have a counter interest i.e. jealousy, their own failure or a co-conspirator.

For example, your friend is a great parent, has a great relationship with his or her partner and is raising his or her good kids. You are having some concerns about your stepchildren and you think, "Let me speak with my friend." Good or bad idea? This will depend on the mindset of your friend.

Good, if your friend can listen and advise you based on the words you are saying and your situation with your step-parenting concerns, but keep in mind that this person may have little or no basis to give educated advice.

Bad, if your friend is going to listen with interruptions all based on their exclusive parenting experiences. Exclusive equates to:

1. A traditional home where the Mom and Dad are the birth parents raising the children under their roof, supervision and rules since birth.
2. A nontraditional home where the Mom is the birth parent or no children and the Dad has 100% custody of the children. Maternal mom is deceased, has moved on completely in her life or she is not involved at all.
3. A nontraditional home where the Father is the birth parent or no children and the MOM has 100% custody of the children. Paternal father is deceased, has moved on completely in his life or he is not involved at all.

You see on their exclusive parenting experiences will not include external influences from the X factor, partial or full time house rules changing, 3 or 4 different parents' rules, societal stigma of step parenting, guilt association, children's desires for maternal and paternal parents re-united, your desire to be successful, interruptions of your schedule and the fact that you have no legal rights to the children but you have assumed the responsibility, mind you, the benefit lasts only as long as you have the children.

Question: With whom do you share your concerns about issues you may encounter as a stepparent?

Valid question and very reasonable. The answer is not so clear-cut and dry. I found it best to talk to God, tried to seek out reasonable likeminded people and at the same time, tried to keep my primary objective ahead of me (the reason I was in our relationship before the introduction of the stepchildren). More preferably, I spoke with my partner (the biological co-parent – my dream maker - Art).

Answer: A Dream Maker (one who supports, encourages, and believes in the dream of a dreamer)

FACT 06:   *"Do not share your dream with a non-dreamer; they may be a Dreamtaker" jrn*

Question: Have you ever been so excited about your dreams that you could not wait to go to sleep?

This story can be found in the book of Genesis of the Holy Bible Chapter 37, and a copy of the text is located in the appendix.

Dream Maker

You and your partner have decided to make a life together and form a new blended family that includes children from one or both of your previous relationships. You may not have had any previous children like myself. Well, congratulations are in order to each of you for taking the next step toward your happiness.

You both desire to make this relationship good and to make this relationship the right one. You both have your minds and hearts set to make this relationship into a blended family. GET READY! GET SET! GO! And you are off to make sure this relationship does not end up like the last one, but it will be a successful one – the best one. You both are the highlights of each other's worlds.

The road ahead of you both can be rewarding, challenging, exhausting and an energetic experience. There is no set clock to tell you both how long or how short a time it should take before you both can proclaim your blended family is a family that blends well. So we suggest you both take off your time tables of expectations and recognize the road ahead may hold deceptions, infatuations, tears and cheers.

FACT 07: It will take time for your new blended family to begin to feel comfortable and function like the well-oiled machine that you both desire.

If you are the parent of the children in this new blended relationship, you are likely to approach remarriage, cohabitation and a new blended family with great joy and expectations. However, your kids or your new spouse's kids (if applicable), their stepparent, your X, the father of the new spouse or significant other, or family members may not be nearly as excited: Why?

- There may be feelings of uncertainty about the upcoming changes and how they will affect relationships with their natural parents.
- They may be concerned about living with new stepsiblings, whom they may not know well or worse ones they may not even like (if applicable).
- There may be questions about your loyalty or devotion to them because now it will be shared.
- Discipline
- Money

- Time
- House Rules
- Expectation
- Differences in family
- Support
- Lack of Support
- Understanding
- Lack of Understanding
- How to say "NO"
- When to say "YES"

There is a story in the Bible in the book of Luke, Chapter 1, that I think is a great example of whom to share your dreams or concerns. This story is about a lady and her cousin. The names of these two women are Mary, the mother of Jesus, and Elizabeth, the wife of Zachariah.

In this story, Mary, the virgin mother of Jesus, had just learned from the angel that she would become pregnant and the angel also told her that her cousin Elizabeth was pregnant in her old age (beyond 60 years of age). Mary and Elizabeth's stories were not identical yet they both had some major similarities: Both became pregnant from miracles and they both were standing in places that other women had not been placed. Sure, other women had become pregnant but not in the manner in which Mary and Elizabeth had become pregnant. I can imagine they both had their share of gossip talkers and corner-of-the-eye watchers, but together they could recognize their similarities – I will say – their "blessing" together and forgo, at least while they were together, the "messing" of others.

Like-minded or like-situated people are the people with whom you want to discuss your step parenting concerns. You may consider speaking with your partner, but they may not have read this book or had the hindsight to be insightful about the role you are playing as a stepparent.

I can just imagine the confusion, fear and unsaid thoughts that Mary must have had in her mind: thoughts about herself, her family, her fiancé, her life and her willingness to do the will of God as she had been honored.

You may experience similar emotions, and your desire is to reach out and seek help. Here is the way I envisioned Mary's conversations went. What if the Virgin Mary decided she must talk to someone, anyone, her single girl friends, family or even her fiancé? And say something like:

"Hey. Guess what! Girl or Babe, you will never believe what happened to me. I was on my way home from work earlier and this angel stopped me told me I was highly favored, the Lord is with me and I would be blessed among women. He told me I would conceive in my womb and bring forth a son and then, I became pregnant. I did not even have to subject myself to a man. Nope, I am just as pure as the day I was born."

Their response, "Really, Mary, of all the things you could say – what? – You don't want to be married to Joseph. The decision has been made and the dowry paid! Did you say you are with child?"

Joseph's response, "Really, Mary, of all the things you could say – what? – You don't want to be married to me. The decision has been made and the dowry paid! Did you say you are with child?"

Mary could reply, "You don't believe me. Well, the angel even told me that my cousin Elizabeth is pregnant in her old age. We all know she has been barren and that is not very good even if Zachariah did not divorce her and get himself a younger wife so he can have a son."

Their response, "Hush girl! Now tell us the truth. Who's the daddy?

Joseph's response, "Mary slow down tell me again what you just told me because I don't think I heard you correctly or I must have misunderstood what I heard you say! Did you say you are with child?"

Mary was wise enough to know who to share her concerns with.

After Mary was gifted with the baby Jesus, the Bible says she arose and went into the hill country with haste. Why do you think Mary went to the hill country with haste?

*[39] At that time Mary got ready and hurried to a town in the hill country of Judea, [40] where she entered Zechariah's home and greeted Elizabeth. [41] **When Elizabeth heard Mary's greeting, the baby leaped in her womb, and Elizabeth was filled with the Holy Spirit.** [42] In a loud voice she exclaimed: "Blessed are you among women, and blessed is the children you will bear! [43] But why am I so favored, that the mother of my Lord should come to me? [44] As soon as the sound of your greeting reached my ears, the baby in **my***

womb leaped for joy. [45] Blessed is she who has believed that what the Lord has said to her will be accomplished!"

Mary went to the home of her cousin Elizabeth, and from what I interpret, she was not expected but the unexpected happened. That is, when Mary greeted her cousin Elizabeth, Elizabeth's baby that had been still for 6 months, leaped for joy. WOW! Someone, who understands your plight and has similar understanding of your situation, has the making of a really good time and could possibly make your baby jump (Dream makers will have a better understanding of your situation and the commonality will stand out). Time may escape you just as it may have with Mary. She stayed three months before returning home.

This is why you want to share your dreams with a dreamer. Sharing your dreams with a dreamer or a likeminded person may give your dreams life and make your dreams (baby) leap for Joy!

If you choose unwisely with whom to share your dream (to live happily ever after with your new blended family), it could be the death of your relationship, your successful step parenting, and you may fall prey to the DREAMTAKER.

Remember the story of Joseph, the dreamer. He got thrown into a well, sold into slavery, told to be dead to his father, accused and jailed all because he shared his dream, which was misunderstood by his brothers.

A more practical example involving money. Consider the following scenarios:

I. If you had only $20.00 in your possession, you are the only one that knows you have this $20.00. You were told that this $20.00 was all the money you would receive for the next two weeks and it also had to cover four other people. You would have to stretch and manage this $20.00 to take care all of your immediate needs and wants and four other people's immediate needs and wants.

II. If you were given another $20.00 which had to be managed among four other people and yourself, and the four other people knew that you have the money. They are in your listening ear sometimes and the other time, they are able to listen to someone else. However, you are to make sure that this shared $20.00 takes care of all of your immediate needs and wants and the four other people's immediate needs and wants.

Do you think the first given $20.00 (I) would be much more manageable than the second $20.00 (II)?

In the first scenario, you have total control. No one knows about it except you, the absence of interference or interpretation of your managing the money. The second scenario, you do not have total control, but you have the money. The involvement of other people, who may not understand your intentions or strategies, may cause of the money to get lost or be mismanaged long before the two weeks are up. Now, why would this happen?

Because the other people's needs, wants or whatever could come into play may it be physically or verbally then you will not have complete control of the money.

They could say *it was mine, I have rights to it, I need this or that, and I have more control over spending than you*. They fear you are going to spend it on yourself, lose it, and become victim of theft or that you might not fully understand their needs.

If you share your dreams with a non-dreamer or dream taker, then you may lose your dream due to the lack of understanding, jealousy, greed, mishap, false agendas, insecurities, or lack of experience. The dream taker wants to take your dream away. The dream maker will be in support of your dreams.

Remember your goals and keep in mind the following three points when sharing your stepparent concerns:

1. Be willing to listen to advice.
2. Be willing to accept advice.
3. Be willing to ignore advice.

The X-Factor

No matter how hard you work on household harmony within your own four walls, research shows that one of the primary sources of children's problems after a divorce is the inability of parents to keep their negative feelings about their ex (or their ex's new partner) to themselves. "Remember, children take their emotional cues from their parents," says Engel. "Negative comments about what goes on in that other household just makes it harder on your kids," she adds. (http://www.ekccc.org/uploads/1/5/0/8/15089416/navigating_the_challenges_of_blended_families.pdf)

In our firsthand experiences, hearsay and other people's stories, speaking negatively about the other parent in front of the children in one word is unacceptable. The word *unacceptable* defined is not pleasing or not welcomed. This chapter is the first wave of what can easily be misinterpreted, as "this is my expected responsibility," "my fatherly duties or my motherly duties."

[Art's 20-20 Hindsight: Clear and Present Dangers]

"Divorce" is complex and really boils down to a decree awarding you and your X the honor to live separate lives. In my case, my X took it upon herself with the support of the court and most of society to make sure that kids fell under her responsibility or roof (the very roof that I assisted in choosing and financially supported) for whatever her reasons may have been.

In other words (IOW), she forced the courts to award her the children in the name of money, love or the fact that all children should be with the mother, but I got the bills and other things dropped on me plus I had to move out. My life had to be downsized to an apartment, not to mention the fact that I thought I was a better parent to our children and I desired to be our children's primary custodial parent. In our case and maybe yours, if your X was awarded custody, even if you both have joint custody, but they have them the majority of the time, I believe that the courts are declaring that the normal day-to-day responsibilities go to her, the custodial parent. If you are not sure which is your case, here is a big hint: if you are paying child support and not receiving it, then the day to day responsibilities of the children belong to the person receiving the child support.

So the basic setup could be explained like this: suppose you both lived in different states, for example, you currently live in Atlanta, Georgia, and she lives in Dallas, Texas, you will not be able to, although you may be willing, make an 800+ mile trip to take your children to the doctor or dentist for a regular visit, but your only avenue of being paternal is to send money in the form of child support and health insurance as ordered by the court and occasional extras.

This was just the paternal drive in me – "I will do anything for my children" or "I will go to the ends of the earth and the moon for my children." But this is understandably not something you can do if you both lived in separate states.

The scenario mentioned above is an example of how you will not be able to respond to unacceptable requests. This responsibility is assigned to the custodial parent but it is not defined or agreed to by you. Your legal responsibility is to pay the child support and maybe a few other things as defined in your divorce settlement. (Make sure you understand your divorce settlement. Take the time to read every line of your divorce decree then get understanding. Make no assumptions.)

Anything that you do beyond this is now considered a charitable act or going beyond what is expected of you and clearly these things should be your choice – not a demand or insistent request. Even if you do these things, it does not mean it will make your X more understanding of your plight to be all that you can be or have to become to your children.

Even if you live in the same state, sometimes there is an invisible boundary that can manifest itself in a variety of ways stopping you from enjoying your children, interfering with your current relationship or just over burdening you.

[20-20: End]

So let's identify the perspective in the standard framework as the co-parent. The co-parent in this book will be the biological parent to the children of the blended family.

Your perspective is that they are your children and they are your responsibility and yes, you want to be a part of the development of your children and that is a normal expected response. However, the X may be under the impression that the co-parent will have to do these extra, added on things and may try to push their responsibilities on to you with increasing frequency, sometimes to the point of demanding you to do them and may even throw in a threat just to give it a little extra kick.

In your mind, you may not see the X's attitude coming at you because you may expect to deal with a little drama. Overlooking the drama is something that you are willing to do based on normal expected thoughts and feelings "I love my children, I am the father, I am the parent also, I want and will do what is best for them and it is not going to hurt anything if I do it just this once." You may not even realize that there is any drama or that you are being imposed upon.

These requests are one-sided demands on you, and it is believed that you will comply because you are at a vulnerable state of mind and you want to be as significant in your children's lives as possible.

This singularly important ideology, that you desired to have your children with you and you want to spend as much time with them whenever opportunity arises, will cause you to comply without considering that you are being imposed on.

I am going to assume that no parent planned to get married, have children, then divorce and have their children placed in a separate home away from their leadership, guidance, and love.

If your X actually respected you as a responsible parent, you would not get unacceptable requests or demands on your time during your scheduled visitation as if you have no life or are not capable of making your own family plans, especially when you do not have the children for legal visitation. If your X respected you as the responsible parent, he or she would actually have to be independent, self-sustaining and responsible person to feel that way and even consider that you may deserve to live a decent life and develop a new fulfilling relationship. After all, you are divorced.

It would be nice but some of the X factors are actually "on the take" and may have subtle malicious, imposing and intrusive intentions. The thinking process may be, at least in my case, "I got the kids and the co-parent needs to do everything else."

This malicious, imposing or intrusive behavior can grow to a point of exasperation, demolition style destruction to your new relationship and to your life. You will have no control of the agenda or your time if you fall into the "honey-do list" that is or has been planned by the X. Without your awareness and even under your nose, this could lead to feeling of loss of control from your stepparent.

[Art's 20-20 Hindsight: Visitation Abuse]

My expectations of weekend visitations with the kids would start on Friday and end sometimes on Sunday with the usual court defined every other weekend schedule. In my premature divorced mind, I favored "the more, the better" concept. If the X-factor was not such an issue, this would be something to think about, but because of the X-factor, I should not have even gone down that path, a lesson that I painfully learned.

Here are the X-factor issues to address:

- X wanted to overburden me to affect my relationship by pushing the kids on us every possible opportunity.

- X wanted to teach Jay a lesson on being a parent since Jay had no children.

- X wanted to reap the benefits of child support but off load the burden of the children.

- X made sure there was a little extra work to do like (homework, library adventures, hair appointments [unfinanced], etc.)

- X wanted extra freedom from the kids so she could have romantic interludes (if she wanted freedom), just give up the child support and the kids – not just the kids.

- X made sure there was a delay when I went to pick up the kids.

- X made sure the time with the kids was irregular by asking for them to be picked up on Saturday, then pick them up on the following Friday but be back on Saturday and the pattern went on from there, stating that they didn't stay the whole weekend.

How do you stop this and gain some respect:

- Don't pick up the kids for a while. Skip a couple of weekends until she gets the message. It is not mandated that you have visitations every other weekend on the clock, but she may believe that to be case and try to use that false information. Child support does not change if they are with the blended family 365 days of the year or not—painful for you and the children but it is a must do in order to give the X the needed attitude adjustment.

- When you do pick them up, only wait 10 – 15 minutes for them to come out. If they are not out in 10 or 15 minutes, leave. Get them on another weekend. The X factor is very much aware that they are supposed to have the children ready for pickup not getting ready.

- If they come to you unprepared, send them back up unprepared

- If the children have appointments on your scheduled weekend or the appointment, skip that weekend.

- If the kids are sick, don't pick them up. It could make others sick.

Since the X factor made it clear in the divorce that they wanted to keep the kids (money), let them. In my X's mind, my time and relationship was not important, and she had the weekend plans to live "big life" at my expense. I eventually began to turn the tables on her. If she wanted to burden me, I made sure she was burdened instead.

[20-20: End]

Imagine you and the new stepparent are in your car. You are in the driver's seat, but your steering wheel, brakes and accelerator are not working for you. They are going to only places that your X planned, and they will only respond to your X's control. It is as if your X is remotely controlling your car and maybe you. Now ask yourself, "Are you being remotely controlled?"

Now, place yourself in the passenger seat but not as yourself but as the stepparent, the lovely or handsome, trusting and interesting person you met a year ago. Can you see what they will see in this circumstance?

Imagine that the both of you were on your way out to a planned dinner, a dinner with candle lights and soft music, but the phone call you just got said with a frantic but firm voice that your son's bed is broken and you need to come and fix it. Without thinking, you make a U-turn to go do this because you know what is wrong with it and it is simple to fix. It will only take a minute.

What will your stepparent think? That incident is not something you need to respond to immediately. Sounds cruel but you really do not need to respond to that at this particular moment in time.

First of all, you had plans, you committed to the plans, you were in the process of executing those plans and they were great plans, but you allowed a non-emergency call to change your plans and the stepparent's mood as well. Your X should have been responsible enough to handle this situation without imposing on you and the stepparent, and that is exactly what your stepparent will see.

The stepparent may think there will be no end to this and get frustrated with you. You are being indirectly controlled and everything that goes on in the other house finds a way to impact you and the stepparent at the most inopportune time.

When you and your X were married, these types of things happened, and you may have handled them or arrangements were made to get it handled. Now that you are divorced and attempting to start a new life, the playing field is different. The X factor will conveniently think it is your turn to handle the non-emergencies like medical checkups, dental appointments and other tasks like track practice, band practice, sports practice or after school tutoring because he or she did it last time as if it were a shared responsibility or if you are still married or in a committed relationship to each other.

The roles of husband and wife should be significantly different between a divorced man with children and a divorced woman with children. If you are married, it is understood that arrangements will be made for pickups and drop offs to best suit the family. This arrangement and understanding was lost when divorce WON. Realizing that the new understanding is that you are a beast of burden and you will have no life and furthermore no aspiring relationships.

The first step to putting brakes on this kind of unacceptable behavior is RECOGNITION. Requests should not be demanded, expected or even desired. You should be awarded the opportunity to choose if the task is something that you and/or your stepparent would like to perform.

Yes, the stepparent should have a voice in this as well which may not go over very well with the X, but that may be because you "don't deserve a life" in their eyes. The upside of that should be recognition of the fact that you are going beyond your newly imposed responsibility as a divorced person with children and these deeds should not go unappreciated.

If your X appears to be unappreciative and looks toward you and your deeds as if this is what you are supposed to do because you are the parent to the children, then they have just been demoted from the mother of my children to "baby mama" with an underlining agenda - DRAMA.

Now consider what a stepparent could be feeling in the above stated scenario. How do you think or have you even thought about what kinds of feelings a stepparent may be feeling when he or she witnesses you being remotely driven by your X?

It is 11:30 pm and you are receiving phone calls from your X for the fifth night demanding that you speak with your children about chores they neglect to do that she had assigned to them in the custodial house.

Let's consider some facts:

➢ The children do not reside in the home with you and their stepparent
➢ You did not assign the chores (these chores may be newly assigned after divorce)
➢ The hour of the call (Inconsiderate)
➢ The number of times the call has been placed (Intrusive)
➢ Inconsiderate of your time, your life and your plans
➢ Demonstrating to you that there is a loss of control
➢ Maybe trying to inflect feelings of guilt for the decision you both made
➢ You don't live there any more
➢ You won't expect your X to fix problems that you have at your current home or apartment

Secondly, let us restate your goal here which is to build 2 stable homes but you are only head of one. You should not be expected to control or manage the house that you had to leave behind and that you are no longer the head.

If the children are not diagnosed special needs, it is time to put some major brakes on the currently displayed "X factor with children behavior." If the children are of special needs, then the custodial parent needs to seek professional guidance on how to handle this situation.

Here are some tips on how to manage the unacceptable requests and help you to increase the respect that should be given and remove the remote control appendage:

❖ Stop the phone calls.
❖ If the calls are going to happen, make sure they are in a respectful hour but keep in mind that the call should be of a real need and most needs are not emergencies.
❖ Provide hours to place the call unless emergency (we will define emergency).
❖ Demand respect for yourself, your life, and your new relationship.
❖ Stress the point that she/he is a parent and she/he needs to act like one.
❖ Inform her/him that you will direct, instruct and demonstrate when the children are in your care to the same standard or degree that you expect her/him to do.
❖ Coach her/him in the directive of what type of calls she/he needs to be placing to you and your home.

These acts are all subliminal actions to keep you under their control, keep you at arm's reach, deny your freedom (requested or not) to have a new full life and to make you feel guilty and overburdened. We have barely touched the surface of what kinds of things that are considered to be unacceptable requests and some of them may not appear to be unacceptable, but when you consider the impact on you, your life, your blended family, your time and the stepparent, they are unacceptable.

In my personal experience, when I had my kids for visitation and placed a call to my X, she would not even answer the phone. That's right! She would call my phone, the children's cell phone repeatedly like it is an emergency as big as a plane flying into the World Trade Center and would be so pissed if we did not answer her call. She never called Ms. Jay's phone which would have been the respectful act to perform. I assume she knew what was going to happen, but she would not answer my call even if I left a message. Understand that the scales are always going to be balanced with your actions and unbalanced with the X's actions in her/him favor. Have you ever noticed that the scales to represent JUSTICE are not equal? Well, I have and I can tell you that image stayed in my mind often of how she could do but did not act the same if I was the one doing the same.

Consider this, "What do you think the X would do if the situation was reversed where you had custody of the kids and you made phone calls to him/her for things that you could clearly handle and you called them at any time of the day or night while knowing that the X was in a commented relationship?" She/he would not even answer the phone, but YOU will be in line for an ear full and a strong "blessing out."

This brings us to another important point and a great way to consider good or problem X behavior. That is to say, "What would be different if you had the kids and the X was awarded visitation?"

First of all, life would be incredibly different for you and your blended family. You would get to keep the money you earn and you might get child support from the X. You would have the desired chore to raise your children directly and first hand. You would not get unacceptable requests, especially at inconvenient times, and you would never make an unacceptable request of the X.

How about this fact? You would be able to be at the activities of your children because you got the schedule when you signed your child up for the sport.

What about when the bed breaks? Not only would you fix it, but you would stop the children from jumping on it. You would be able to enforce household rules and make sure these rules are respected any place the children are whether you are present or not.

Think about why there would be such a difference. You would not be intrusive because you would just handle your business and your X would not be part of it.

Let me introduce Jeff and Donna, a couple's dilemma – Unacceptable Request.

Jeff and Donna have been seeing each other for about a year now and they get along very well. Jeff is an electrical engineer and Donna works for the Department of Energy. Together, they are like a well-oiled machine as compatible couples are with each being the other's compliment and enjoying each other's company.

Everything was sailing on smoothly until they were hit with unexpected, unplanned and unannounced X factor drama with children.

It is Thursday and Jeff is at work. Jeff receives a phone call from his X informing him that Daniel, their 11 year old son, needs a haircut since he will be taking school pictures on Monday which is in a couple days, and she can't take him any time soon because she has to take the other two sons to football practice. She has been working late; her boss does not like her and may want to fire her. Besides that she took him to get a haircut the last time.

Not thinking and a little distracted by the load of negativity, trying to continue his efforts at work and in order to get back to work quickly, Jeff agrees to take Daniel to get a haircut.

The next day, the X after seeing that Jeff was willing to take Daniel to get a haircut, decides since Daniel will be with his dad, it would be a good opportunity for Daniel to get a new pair of basketball shoes. The pair that Daniel has is getting a little ragged and he has been asking about a pair of Nike's that he has seen in the shoe store.

Jeff planned on taking Daniel to get the haircut after work on Sunday, before he has to take the kids home. He was thinking that he and Donna have no special plans on that day. He gives Donna a call to tell her about his new task. Donna does not have a problem with it and thinks it won't take that long and he will be home in time for dinner.

Before they could hang up, Jeff gets a call on the other line and it is his X. He tells Donna that he will call her back in a few minutes.

The X drops another long-winded request telling Jeff that since he will have Daniel he could take Daniel to get a new pair of basketball shoes, too. Jeff says ok … he will do it. He calls Donna back and explains the new task. He added that his X said she would give Daniel the money for the shoes, but she asked if he could pay for Daniel's haircut.

Donna is not in disagreement but she is starting to wonder if anything else is going to be dropped on Jeff by his X. She has seen this pattern before and she now knows the signs. She also is aware of the fact that the school notifies parents in more than enough time to have their children ready for picture day. Not to mention two weeks prior, Daniel needed new dress shoes that conveniently fell on Jeff.

Sunday arrives without any additional phone calls or new tasks. Jeff and Daniel make it to the barber and then to the shoe store. Jeff is trying to rush so he can get home at a decent time. It takes him 30 minutes to get home from the X's house.

While Jeff and Daniel are at the shoe store, Jeff asked Daniel if his mother gave him any money for the shoes. Daniel replies that she didn't give him any money. Jeff was thinking that he didn't want to waste a trip so he decided to just pay for the shoes and call it a day.

Before Jeff could get to the checkout line, he gets another call. It is the X. Jeff is starting to wonder if she can see him. The phone calls are timed so perfectly.

She is now asking Jeff if he could pick up a pizza that she ordered which was just down the street from the house. Jeff's thinking "what the heck," he is already near the pizza place. He hastily tells her, "No problem," but he forgot to ask about the money for the shoes and to ask if she arranged to pay for the pizza.

Jeff and Daniel arrived at the restaurant to pick up the pizza. He finds out that no arrangements had been made to pay for the pizza, and the order was called in 3 minutes before he walked in. Now, Jeff is getting a little angry as well a little tired from all of the add-on tasks plus the speed which his money is leaving his pocket. He says to himself, he will get the pizza this time but there won't be a next time.

When he arrives that the X's house, she meets them at the door and asked if he could step in the house for a minute. He says okay wondering if there is something broken in the house.

She says that their other son David needs some help with his math homework that he has been having problems with this class for a while. Jeff is thinking why she would ask him to do this at the last minute. After all, it has been a long day and it seems to keep getting longer. He was tired and ready to go home.

Jeff gives Donna a call to say that he will be home a little later because he has to help David with a homework assignment.

Donna says that she thought he would have been home sooner and a couple of their friends stopped by to see them. They were still waiting for him to arrive. Donna, being a little embarrassed by having to tell their guests that they are not going to see Jeff, asked what else he had to do.

Jeff explained about the haircut: the barber was slow and had three other guys before he could get to Daniel and no appointment had been made. He further explains about having to buy the shoes because the X forgot to give Daniel the money.

He told her about the pizza that was to be ordered right away but was ordered a few minutes before he got there, and he ended up paying for that, too. He explained about David's needing help with his homework and if he didn't get help, he might not get a good grade in that class and this was told to him as he was dropping Daniel off.

Donna's "what else will be dropped on Jeff by his ex-wife nightmare" has come to maturity. She sees that Jeff, just as before, has fallen for the "baby mama" tricks again. She knows that Jeff is the non-argumentative type and will not raise a fuss unless he is really angry and she knows that his X knows this, too.

The X has successfully taken over Jeff in a short time by getting him to do things that she should have done herself. On any other day, how were she and the kids eating and getting homework help?

This type of dilemma happens to many non-custodial parents with children and it may look like there is no underlying motive by the X other than convenience. This may be true but it should not happen this way. The X has the indirect pleasure of disrupting the co-parent's plans and life by causing him to be a convenient "gopher" not caring about inconveniences to him.

The new stepparent will see these intrusions as problems if the X continues to take control of his time by making him too busy to carry out any of his own plans. It is time to make sure the X realizes that since she agreed to keep the kids and the house, there are some responsibilities that go with that.

A custodial parent along with the newly blended family would handle these responsibilities without needing help from his X whereas the X will attempt to push them onto the co-parent. The co-parent will have to make these types of unacceptable requests stop if he wants to develop a successful blended family.

If the X makes plans for the children and expects the co parent to carry them out because she had some other activity to handle, this does not mean it is an emergency. A lack of planning on their part does not mean an emergency for you.

In some cases, it may be suitable to let the X's calls go to voicemail and if it is important enough, they will leave a message. At that point, you can decide if this is something that you need to give attention to. Do not fear saying "no." You have every right to be able to say "No."

In any case, if the X asks you do to anything that requires payment of some sort, make sure the money is provided. Otherwise, you will in fact be indirectly paying extra child support and they may just conveniently decide to forget to give you the money. They will continue to milk you for money and plan to keep the child support money for non-child expenses.

Now let us take you behind the scene to see how the X can use all of these phone calls and requests to work, not only against your time and money but also to manipulate the child's thinking about you making the child see things differently instead of how they really are.

Let's suppose that the X is making two of the three calls placed (the one for the haircut and the basketball shoes) in front of the child and he hears the mom's explanation about the haircut and the request for the shoes with the added notation that she would pay the money back for the shoes and you pay for the haircut.

In the child's mind, he may be thinking, yes, you should have taken him to get the NIKE basketball shoes, but his mom really paid for them because she was going to give you the money back. The pizza was already paid for if the child did not pay attention to the end of the transaction, and if you did pay, then the mom was going to also give you the money back. It could look like that is fair – mom takes some financials and dad makes some and besides, he is taking care of another family anyway. The child may not be any wiser that the Dad is paying support, insurance, etc., and these types of needs are covered under the child support money.

On the other side, your blended family has been pushed to the back burner for no good reason. The guests arrived and left without your presence, the blended family had to put on a good face and hide their true emotions in front of company and you, at least, while you were away handling someone else's business.

The payback money never happened and it was not even followed up with a decent thank you.

If you pull the shade up, you may recognize that you just got played. That is right! You allowed your past to interrupt your present, which may in turn have a big impact on your future. Remove your shades co-parent and keep a sharp eye open for the X factor and any games that may be thrown your way.

Leftovers

There is a story in the Bible, in the book of Mark that speaks about Jesus feeding a multitude of 5000 with seven loaves of bread and a few fish. The multitude had been following Jesus and the disciples for three days and Jesus wanted to feed them so they would not faint on their return journey home.

After the miracle meal of feeding this many with so little, there were seven baskets of leftovers. They started out with not enough and ended up with more than enough.

Just imagine three days of seminars, traveling around place to place, sleeping on rock beds, walking through dirt roads with dust flying everywhere in open-toed shoes, dirt getting in between your toes – ugh. That in itself is frustrating. Then trying to feed everyone, clean up and catch the next ship out – in a word "exhausting!" Now increase the drama, aboard the ship – the haters are on the ship trying to tempt Him with questions of no significance, like getting on a plane or bus wishing only to rest from your trip and you get a smelly talking person next to you with a hyperactive kid.

This story is a great prelude into a personal encounter that I had with my stepson. You see, when I tell you that I had the help of "DIVINE insight" and "DIVINE hold-your-tongue-before-you-speak" to the words that came out of his mouth, nobody told me, "GIRL, you are going to have to deal with the children_and the X saying ugly things to you!"

I can only give credit to God, not just on this one occasion but on several occasions, as I journeyed through the trials of becoming a good stepparent. God saved the day!

The words that I was able to share with my stepchildren during these encounters were not rehearsed; nobody told me of a similar incident, I did not pre-think of what I was going to say or do and I did not have a book like Lethal Weapon to give me a road map of scenarios. How could I prepare for the unknown?

After a stressful week at work and the anticipation of what will the weekend bring knowing that my stepchildren were scheduled to come, it always was eventful during the following week because of fallout from their visit instigated by the X Factor.

Our son entered the home and he was in a hurry to share something with me. I need to mention that on the last visit, I blocked an undercover game he was trying to run on his father.

We had house rules which flowed in this fashion: greeting first then take all of your things upstairs and remember do not bring any conversation or behavior from the home you're leaving.

Picture this scenario, my stepson and I are in the kitchen alone getting a soft drink for him and a bottle of water for me and he said to me, "Ms. Jay, my momma says you have her leftovers."

I had tried to tell Art on several occasions that my name, character and anything about me was being served up in their mom's household as rubbish and so was he. At this time, he was not into believing me. He was wearing dark- mind glasses, the ones with a sticker attached "I do not want to believe she would do that" blinders.

I replied, "What did you say?" (Totally, disregarding one of the house rules) so he repeated as he was sipping on a cold drink that I purchased. "My momma says, "You got her leftovers."

My approach was quite calm because I was always expecting something out of the way on their weekend. It was a perfected practice on their part and acceptance on mine.

I responded "**Leftovers!** Do you know what **leftovers** are?" ... He was looking at me all smug like a cat that just ate the canary.

No response from him; I said, "**Leftovers** are the 'special' at the restaurant for the next day. They become the ENTRÉE – the main course. Did you know that Goodwill stores are a million dollar business based on leftovers? Let me tell you how Goodwill works. You see people give to Goodwill the items they no longer want and then Goodwill processes the items and then sells them to people who desire to pay for their asking price".

He was just looking at me now. His posture had changed from standing upright to leaning on the counter top. I responded "Did you know that this water I am drinking was left over from the Creations of time?"

"What?" he says.

I responded "That is correct. There is not any new water. It just has been processed, recycled, flavored, fluoride, purified, enhanced and re-marketed."

Now that I had his attention, a few coins on the counter drew my attention. I said, "You like money, right?" "Okay, so get four quarters off that counter." And he did. I asked him, "So do you think your father loves me?"

He responded, "Yes!"

I said, "Put a quarter on the other side of the counter." I then asked, "Do you think your sister loves me?"

He replied, "Yes, sometimes".

I said, "Okay, I will take that. Put another quarter on the side of the counter with that one". Then I asked, "Do you love me?

He replied, "Yeah," shyly, but he said yeah.

"Okay. Then put another quarter on the counter with the other 2."

He did. I looked at the quarters. I said, "There are 3 in one stack and one in the other stack". I ask him which of the stack had more value; he naturally chose the one with the 75 cents.

Then I said to him, "Let me see … I got you, your sister and your father; that makes 75 cents. Seventy-five cents is greater than 25 cents. Looks like I am winning. That is what I do—win!" I then proceeded to say, "I would rather be **leftover**" pointing at the set of 3 quarters "than **left behind,**" pointing at the 1 quarter.

I had made a diligent effort not to speak negatively about their mother or entertain any of her ignorance; however, on this day, **I spoke before I choked** on my response. I said to him, "I generally do not entertain ignorance, but I want you to know if your father is a leftover then you and your sister are also. You all were leftovers from divorce and that includes your mother."

I said, "I am a leftover." He raised his eyebrow. Then he spoke, "You were never divorced or had any children."

Then I said, "From my mother's afterbirth." (I wanted to say, "and your mom has been left over from a broken heart. I can't see how your father ever worked with her. She is left behind in her own mess she created" - but I did not ☺).

My next response was directed and intended to stop any more insulting messages from crossing my threshold, at least, by him. I said, "You see, Son, your mother did not even realize she had a good piece of fruit, forgo it being a lemon. She is bothered that I was able to take the fruit, call it her lemon and make my own peach lemonade. I have raised the bar of life in you, your sister and your father." My stepson was speechless. I then asked him to take his things upstairs and get ready for us to go out to dinner.

You may have thought WOW - that was creative. Well, it certainly was a Peter moment. A Peter moment, at least by my definition, is when you have been granted the right answer and you had no knowledge of its accuracy or how you guessed the correct answer.

As referenced in the Bible, the story in the book of Mark when Jesus ask the disciples "who do you say I am," the disciples were throwing out answers and Peter said it correctly. Then Jesus responded that his Father in heaven gave Peter the answer.

To add fuel to the fire that evening, we all went to dinner and upon entering the restaurant, the special for the evening was posted, and my son responded, "That is what I would like to have tonight."

We all ordered. Ladies first, then son, then the father – teaching skills in and out of the home. After everyone had ordered, I asked the waitress, "How does the chef or the restaurant come up with the special of the day?"

She responded, "Oh the chef just uses whatever is good that is **left over** from the previous day!"

I looked up at my stepson (who I had come to think of as my son) and he was already looking at me. I mouthed to him "Win! That is what I do!"

Did that put a nail in his coffin of bringing X factor messages to try to tempt me to be more like his mother? Yes! To this day, seven years later, I have not had to entertain any ignorant messages from him from his mother. I am sure that conversations and comments continued about "us," but they do not come to me via him. Thank GOD!

In this case, the following inklings could have been the intent's special delivery. Maybe my son wanted to share the thoughts of his mother about me? Maybe he was rationalizing to himself that he could use this as a way of looking to get me to step down from my chosen position? Perhaps he thought it would give him the upper hand if I felt lower about myself or my position in his father's life?

I cannot answer how he was feeling or why he chose to bring that garbage to our home. At that moment in time, I did not care and I still do not care, nor did I ask him why he selected to share that statement with me.

He was 13 years old, and he was old enough to discern that his comment was not a compliment. At least, that's what he thought when he presented it to me, but you see how God changed his mother's statement about his dad into a compliment for me, his dad and them. He is now a very talented and artistic young man that thinks before he speaks.

Important: I did share the conversation with his father, asking him not to say anything directly about it to our son. I shared it because I wanted him to accept the fact that he was being trashed in the other home, and I always wanted him to be aware of conversations so that if he was questioned later by the X factor or if he wanted to add or subtract from my input, he was informed and had a voice.

I did share with my stepson when we were alone after dinner this advice: "Be wary of the messenger, be mindful of the message and be attentive of the receiver of the message."

In our house, the children were being shown the positive side of their father, his worth and what he was doing to make their lives better. We both made it a standard practice not to speak negatively about the other parent in front of the children. This was not an easy standard to maintain, but we did it.

The X-factor's trashing of the daddy was not as effective as it had been in the past. So, I guess I became a larger target for her. Well, what she did not realize or she has learned, she would never be able to hit this moving target. I was on a winner's mission, and I was not losing the war.

Did you recognize how I, as the stepparent, had to take a high road despite the hurtful comment? I stayed in the family role, entertained then made time to assist the child in his state of uneasiness for making the uncouth statement. Stepparents are in the position to be harmed if they are not armed.

FACT 08:   ASK – (A)lways (S)eek (K)knowledge. jrn

Learn what your enemies' or your opponents' weapons are, then super charge your Lethal Weapons.

FACT 09:   If you have set a standard for yourself, do not allow substandard behavior or people to have you change your standard.

FACT 10:   "Stand up for the right thing then watch the left fall down." jrn

FACT 11:   Communication is vital to the survival of your relationship with the co-parent of your stepchildren. It will allow you both an opportunity to be aware.

Keeping my eyes on my intimate relationship and continual counting on guidance from my God were my numbers 1 & 2 focal points that assisted me in becoming a successful stepmom.

Package Deal

Have you ever heard the cliché "It is a package deal" or "You knew what you were getting into when you got into that relationship, it was a package deal?"

The definition of package deal as recorded in Merriam Dictionary is *a collection or group related goods or services sold as a unit.* I got all these tools in a package deal for only $39.95. What about giving me all three shirts as a package deal?

It is a term that is used in the business world, particularly in sales. It is also a termed used to describe a woman that is very well shaped.

I used Google and searched for the origin and meaning of this term "Package deal" as it is related to a person with children seeking a new relationship with someone with or without children of their own. I found nothing at all.

The expression "package deal," the cliché, is commonly thought of as a potential mate of a person who is single and has children or a person who is involved with a mate with children or an X. Sometimes a person seeking a mate may refer to himself/herself as a package deal, all implying that they come into the relationship with children.

It takes courage, love and determination to partner with someone who has children and if you have children; you can add another dimension to the picture, if you and your new mate decide to have a child of your own union. This act will really sweeten the deal. It is hard work to be a member of a blended family, the heaviest weight being placed on the person in the step parenting position.

You see, knowing that a "package deal" is the beginning of your new relationship after the union of you and the other parent is dissolved, the horizon may not look so good or certainly not as clear for you if you did not have children.

Knowing that you are walking into the lives of an existing family and understanding the role you will play as first an outsider or the intruder and then the real reason my parents will not get back together are two big separate bears to put into hibernation.

[Art's Hindsight 20-20: No Package Deal]

I never considered that we (my kids and I) were a package deal. To me, a package deal would imply that we are coming as a group, and you have to take the entire group (good, bad or indifferent) or none of us and we move on. I considered myself as a unique individual, and I saw my kids as two other unique individuals each having complete and separate personalities and desires.

Coming into this relationship, you are adding to the group, making us 4 separate individuals. There is no package! I heard the expression "package deal," but I never internalized it. We are all too unique to be considered a package. I never liked package deals anyway.

For example, when you subscribe to a TV satellite service, you are offered packages. The packages have a variety of programming, most of which I will never watch like a shopping channel. I may see 5 to 8 channels out of a package that I may watch, but there are at least 50 other channels I will never watch but have to pay for.

Why can't I just pick the channels that I will watch and pay for what I like as opposed to paying for up to 50+ channels to get the 8 channels that I want? The concept is just wasteful.

By the same token, if you say you and your kids are a package deal, first of all in my opinion, this is another label for "bad deal." Are you trying to cover up some other baggage that no one will ever want to have unless it is a part of a package? Do you think that the only way you will be accepted by another person or family is if you give an all or nothing type of ultimatum?

Sure, you have to take into consideration that you are now a parent with children and you want the best life for your children and yourself, but to decide that if the other person doesn't conform to your expectations and your situation, this is the first step to cancelling any chance of you and your family moving beyond divorce, separation or the absentee parent.

The alternative is to realize that you are a flexible and dynamic individual and you are interested and willing to make the sun shine for someone. You are not coming to the table to be a package deal, but you are setting up a conference and you are ready to negotiate plans to navigate a path to happiness, growth, excitement and an array of selfless devotion. The same principles should be cultured in your children.

[20-20: End]

Okay, so let's talk about this package deal. What exactly are you saying when you term you and your children as a "package deal?"

- Does that mean take it or leave it?
  - In Other Words (**IOW**) – Take me with my children and problems or leave me alone
- Does it mean that you have no options in this relationship?
  - **IOW** – This is my final offer – me and them or no me!
- Does it mean that it is only a one-way street?
  - **IOW** – It will be our way or no way!
- Does it mean you and yours have the right of passage and your new chosen mate is to be at a roadblock, detour or a never-ending crossroad?
  - **IOW** – Accept whatever we bring to the table however we bring it because we are hurting from divorce, separation and loss, so deal with it.
- What if your new chosen mate has children and now you both have package deals?
  - **IOW** – Now what? Who wins the first chair—your kids or mine?
- How does this business deal work out?
  - **IOW** – Win-Win, Win- Lose, Lose-Win or Lose-Lose?
- Which one of the packages gets more of a deal on your time?
  - **IOW** – Choose one – the children out of the blended shared home or the children in the blended home
- Which one of the packages gets left behind?
  - **IOW** – Choose one – In the stepparent's house or custodial parent's house.
- Which one of the packages gets to move forward in front of the other?
  - **IOW** – Choose one – In the stepparent's house or custodial parent's house.
- How are the options and roadblocks determined?
  - **IOW** – What steps are taken to measure what is best for the family?
- If your package is you and your children, what role does the X Factor play?

- - **IOW** – How much control will the X have in the blended home?
- What role will you play in this package?
  - **IOW** – Hurt Father? Recovered Dad? Hurt Mom? Recovered Mom?
- What role do the children get to play?
  - **IOW** – Masters of the relationship? Captain of the Ship? Child of Recovery?
- How long do the children get to play this role?
  - **IOW** – Until healing begins? Until your relationship ends?
- How do you and I agree to the roles that are to be played?
  - **IOW** – Uncle or Aunt? Ice Cream Daddy? Sugar Coat Mommy?
- How do we stop the role of the X Factor from destroying our new package?
- If you are a package deal, what is the bonus prize or discount offered to your new mate?
- When you and your new mate come to a crossroad in your decisions about the package, then where do you go to try to get resolution?
- How can you (co-parent) bring all this so-called package to the table and have no plans for success?
- How do you (stepparent) accept this entire package with no plans for success?
- Where will you go to get the support, compassion or understanding when the packager is not handling his or her package, which denies benefit for you?
- What happens when the packager is torn between their children's guilt, his or her guilt for the loss (separation, divorce or death) of the other biological parent and the stepparent?
- If it is a package deal that is setup by society that you accept him or her with their children, should the bottle spin to the opposite side?
- Should society not automatically expect or demand that he or she and the children accept you? No questions asked! No emotional tasked! Just the understanding that what is good for them is good for you?
- Do you know of any society or creation where the children choose the parents? Where the babies decide who their parents will be?

Sure in the broad sense, in some foster parents or adoptive parenting situations, the children may have a say in the choice of their parents, but the ultimate decision is not of the child. It really is up to the adults.

In the beginning of time, the Father made a man then He created a woman. The woman and the man then procreated children. The children became adults then they procreated children.

Children do not chose their parents; however, parents do make the choice to have children. Some may not have been in ideal situations but the results are the same – the adults had the children. It is a behavior that has been permitted by single–divorced parents with children and they believe this fact even in the traditional family.

Come on now! Do not be shocked by the statement you have heard people speak of "how they did all that they could to make sure that man or lady was not going to replace their mom or dad."

Maybe this one from the children: he or she was "not going to be my parent and I did everything in my power to cause destruction." "The nerve of him or her to think they were going to come up in here and tell me what to do?" "He or she must be out of their mind thinking that some woman or man is going to be acting like Father or Mother to me." "She is too young to be my mother; how is that going to look?" "He is too old to be my father anyway?"

This list could go on for days; however, you get the gist of what is being implied. These hidden and sometimes very obvious agendas are selfish!

Selfish in the fact that these children have taken control and decided your happiness is no longer a consideration. Your relationship with their parent was not successful or their parent's relationship with you was not successful and that will be your punishment for the rest of their lives.

You may even feel that you do not deserve to be happy and in a relationship that could prove to be rewarding for you and your children.

Social ideologies may have you convinced that life will be better if you remained a single parent with children. This may qualify you for a tax break. I can be both mother and father. Heck! You may have been in the role of duality in your previous relationship.

Perhaps you are convinced that your unsuccessful relationship is your punishment or life sentence so it is your new job to make your X mate's life a living hell and help push your children into a position of HATE not Love.

In biblical days, divorce was not as easily attainable; yet being childless in a marriage was not a good thing either. The unspoken rule of the land was to stay together and make children. There was a system of the land to assist female widows and children. The woman became the property of the next man in the family: brother, uncle, cousin, even father.

In today's society, there are some systems in place to assist single parents with children, orphaned children and children whose parents were lost at an early age in the child's life. However, there is no system of protection of the stepparent. The stepparent is not a new position in our human social evolution. It is as old as time according to the book of Genesis and Matthew of the Holy Bible.

You might think if something has been around all this time that some type of legislation would have been in place to protect and serve the persons that are placed in these roles whether voluntary or involuntary. Well, think again; there isn't.

It is like step parenting is a secret hidden in plain sight. Step parenting is known about but not recognized. If you doubt this, go into the store to purchase a card saying "Happy Mother Day Stepmom", "Happy Father Day Stepdad" or order a T shirt that reads "My mom is a StepMOM", or a T shirt that reads, "I am the proud husband to a StepMOM" or "I am the proud wife to a StepDAD" or even, "My kids have a great stepmom or stepdad."

Okay, I know you can buy a mother's day card that says "Happy Mother's Day" or "Happy Father's Day". It works but it's not perfect. There is something special about having a perfect fit rather than just having a good fit.

•

Setting up House

Statistically, research gathered by experts in this field demonstrates it typically takes between two and five years for a blended family to establish itself. This statistic is just that, "a number based on the masses," and it is not absolute. The Internet is so readily available with this information.

For me personally, I cannot qualify how the stats on stepparents are gathered based on the fact the majority of step parenting stats are negative. I am convinced that the statistics are just numbers representing a class of people who do not have my or your new attitude, our will and our new co-parent's mindset which is "We will make our new chosen love work and put forth our best effort to blend our families successfully".

How many times have you filled out an application or questionnaire asking to check the box stepparent? Or completing your taxes and are asked if you have stepchildren living in the home? Or if you are a stepparent to a child? So, I leave you with the question – how are the stats being gathered on stepparents?

Take a moment to review this example of how statistics can be misleading in their presentation of a conclusion as if it has to be factual.

75% more interracial marriages are occurring this year than 25 years ago. Thus, our society accepts interracial marriages.

A major flaw is that we don't have the information that we need to make a reasonable judgment. What is the rate at which marriages are occurring? Suppose only 1% of marriages 25 years ago were interracial and so now 1.75% of marriages are interracial (1.75 is 75% higher than 1). But this latter number is hardly evidence suggesting the acceptability of interracial marriages. In addition, the statistic provided does not rule out the possibility that the number of interracial marriages has seen dramatic fluctuations over the years and this year is not the highest. Again, there is simply not enough information to understand fully the impact of the statistics.
(http://onlinestatbook.com/2/introduction/what_are.html)

So now are you asking yourselves the question how do we begin setting up our new house?

Answer: By planning your work then working your plan! The beginning for everyone can be a rough ride. To make it more realistic, it could be like riding in bumper cars.

[Art's 20-20 Hindsight: Bumper Car Strategy]

When I look back at how we (Jay and I) began to form an alliance (encompassing the kids) against the X factor drama, we put up a logical protective barrier. We needed to ensure that if any drama attempted to rear its ugly head, we were ready to manage it. We made sure that the kids understood and practiced not transferring information between our home and the X's house. We made sure rules of engagement were activated.

This is like when you go to the fair with some of your friends and ride the bumper cars. While you are waiting in line, you begin to work on a strategy with them to intercept any attackers that may target any of you. One of your strategies may be that you plan to position yourself between the attacker and their target before they can get their speed up or you could try to hit them before they make the strike thus breaking down their momentum. Lastly, you call out to your friends to intercept the attacker if they are able get between the attacker and your targeted friend.

If the attackers get too aggressive, you call to the group to signal that it is time for "all-out attack mode" so you and your friends can corner the aggressors and slow them down with a few good bumps.

The rules of engagement for drama can be like riding bumper cars with your blended family (in our case – me, jay and the kids) where you have to work together, demonstrate your collective strength, communications and coordination. You have to do the same with X factor drama. The bottom line is to outsmart the X factor drama (or attackers) and keep it in its place.

[20-20: End]

House rules are the boundaries set up and established for the purpose of creating order, safety, privacy and management of the house. It is important to recognize that house rules are a universal necessity, and it is not limited to just when you become a stepparent. You may not realize it but you have some house rules that may not be posted or are assumed for example, locking the entrance doors at night before bedding down. My parents had a house rule that I did not quite appreciate as a child but now it has shown itself approved by me. The rule was "Do not slam or lock any bedroom doors."

Art is a strong advocate in believing that children need parental consistency and they desire order. He and other experts believe that without the previous, kids can become confused and insecure which can sometimes result in unexpected behavior.

House Rules are not new to man, and yes, this is a correct statement. The very first house that is sited in the book of Genesis certainly had house rules.

God the Father created the first house or estate and called it the Garden of Eden, and He made it home to Adam then Eve. He gave them access to everything and warned of only one thing – the tree of knowledge of good and evil. Now God did not leave them hanging on a dangling rope since he informed Adam of the impending results if they ate from the tree of knowledge that thou shalt surely die if this house rule was broken. According to the KJV bible verse 16.

I am not sure if you are familiar with the story, but I will tell you that the house rule was broken and consequences did happen. Adam and Eve were evicted from the Garden of Eden, their custom designed home, and the relationship that was shared in the garden with the Lord God changed. House rules are required to avoid the bad consequences for the basic step of establishing workable order.

In Genesis 2:8-9, we read: "The LORD God planted a garden eastward in Eden, and there He put the man whom He had formed. (The house) And out of the ground the LORD God made every tree grow that is pleasant to the sight and good for food." Some believe the Garden was atop a mountain, or perhaps it was an outlet for freshwater springs, because we read, "a river went out of Eden to water the garden, and from there it parted and became four riverheads" (<u>*Genesis 2:10*</u>*).*

Genesis 2:16: And the LORD God commanded the man, saying, of every tree of the garden thou mayest freely eat: [17] *But of the tree of the knowledge of good and evil, thou shalt not eat of it: (The Rule) for in the day that thou eatest thereof thou shalt surely die. (The consequence)*

I had the experience of taking the course to become a certified foster parent. In these classes, I learned about the challenges, difficulties and the limitations that were placed on a family desiring to become foster parents to displaced children.

FACT 12:   The benefit of fostering children over step parenting is that as a foster parent, you have rights with the children, but as a stepparent, you have no or very limited rights.

This fact alone is enough to insist and establish house rules for your protection and the protection of your family. I am grateful for the education I received in this program because I was better prepared with the cautions to take once I entered my step parenting role. The law is very limited for stepparents but I can tell you that I was convinced if they could protect a foster parent with or without bloodline and if I stayed in the same boundaries, I should be comparably protected.

I was wrong in this thought after hearing other stepparents' real live stories of how the system did not protect them. However, I was once again blessed in my knowledgeable ignorance.

When Art and I began our journey into blending his family, we did not think to consult the internet or an expert of the subject matter. We just began our lives based on our desires, hoping that our background, influences, love and respect were sufficient, and I sought out divine assistance because I was the one experiencing the greatest change, which was by my choice.

Sure, Art and the children had changes to experience, but their changes were expected since they were the product of divorce.

Experts suggest that you and your partner develop a list of values you both want to teach such as expectations, accountability, responsibility, honesty and respect. Then converse about both of your parenting styles—desired and actual life experiences. This discussion is not a onetime session, and you should allow room for flexibility. Parenting is not rigid or in a solid state like ice. It is and has been since the beginning of time in a state of fluidity so you have to raise the bar a notch when parenting follows the word step i.e., step parenting. It is like driving in fog on a curvy mountain road – cannot see what is coming next!

For example, you may think all children need a set time for going to bed, and adults need to have their time for each other. Your spouse, however, is convinced that those rules should apply during the school and workweek but not the weekend. Well, if this is the rule of the land, you can count out any order or structure of your normal when his kids are visiting. If you have kids and these rules apply seven days, conflict is looking you both directly in the face.

Of course, developing a strategy or the plan seems like child's play compared with working the plan, and it can be particularly difficult for a new stepparent to start laying down the law.

We are convinced that part of the reason for our success rate was establishing house rules prior, during and after the kids' visitation. If we were going to disagree or refute on a decision for the children, we agreed never to appear disagreeable in front of the children.

FACT 13: Do not give the opponent an opportunity to divide and conquer.

When receiving your stepchildren in your home for the first time, they may have a feeling of loss due to divorce of birth parents, friends and their primary home. They may have feelings of guilt, rejection, loneliness, anger, and they may be frustrated over having life disrupted by their parents and now having to deal with another adult that is with the parent that they no longer get to have full time.

Having your stepchildren officially for the first time will probably be exciting for you and frightening for them. Remember, you are meeting these children during one of the most traumatic periods of their lives. This initial meeting is part of the trauma because it signifies more loss and change. It is the first "UN-asked question" answered in their minds – "Mom and Dad are not getting back together".

Making the stepchildren's first few visits in your home as comfortable as possible for them may mean an easier adjustment to step parenting and your family's ways. On the first visit of the official "this is permanent" and you will be a member of our family, the following should be done immediately with follow-up because the children may not remember everything on the first run:

- Offer physical comfort to the children (if appropriate), talk little and accept the feelings that the children may have. A handshake or hug establishes from the beginning the type of greeting you will demand, expect and appreciate.
- Show new children around your home immediately.
- Let the children know that they can come to you for help or to discuss anything and if you cannot answer or help, you will help find someone who can.
- You may want to give the children a special code, or signal for them to use if they have something very important or urgent to tell you.
- Have and point out nightlights in children's room and bathroom.
- Show the children where personal items are kept in the bathroom such as, the children's new toothbrush, toothpaste, towels, washcloths, toilet paper, etc.
- Show the children their beds, closet space and drawers; help children hang up clothes, put away clothes in drawers, if they need and/or want help.
- Point out children's play space.
- Show the children where meals will be hosted. Identify areas of no eating, no trespassing.

Do not celebrate their arrival by inviting interested friends and relatives over for a look at them. Remember, they are sad and hurting inside and may be confused and self-conscious. The stepchildren do not want to be put on display or to see if they will meet the approval of friends or relatives. The children need the security of a regularly scheduled day like regular playtime, naptime and mealtime

Allow the children a few moments or some time alone for adjustment then invite them to common areas with a definite time. But from the beginning, show them that you are in control and they will get in line.

During the first official stay at your home, it is a great time to discuss the house rules. The house rules should be written down and post a copy for them to view.

Remember your house rules may be different from the other parent's home. Everyone in the house without thinking may recognize your current house rules; however, the new children arriving at your home may not remember all the rules the first time.

We suggest posting the house rules prior to the arrival of the children. An example a few of our house rules are listed below:

1. Always greet everybody in the house with a warm greeting upon arrival
2. Take your things up to your room instead of leaving them in the common or family shared area
3. Do not put items in the kitchen refrigerator that you do not want to share with others
4. Never bring conversations or details from the other home to this home
5. Try to see both sides of the equations before you draw conclusions
6. It is always okay to ask a question
7. Respect things and people in this house
8. Respect yourself

On the right side, if you and the father or mother of the children all lived under the same roof all the time, then it would be easier to manage meals, finances, house rules, discipline, rewards, schedules and a host of responsibilities associated with managing a family successfully.

On the left side, if you and the father or mother of the children will not live under the same roof all the time, sometimes you must add in the practices, habits, likes, dislikes, personalities of another adult, more children, different schedules, house rules and responsibilities associated with managing a family successfully.

The right side will come with its own issues; however, the left side's issues will be increased. Acknowledge that first influential relationship (husband, wife, and their children relationship or mom, dad and children) has formed patterns, habits or foundational steps in the following areas: understanding, respect, disrespect, and free time. House rules are set into place, some voluntary and some involuntary, early in the stages of their marriage, cohabitation or transfer visitations from the beginning of raising of their family.

In a blended family, all of the previous listed areas have to be established. The setup of relationships, understanding, respect and house rules are designed after the first influence has occurred whether it was a good or bad, whether it was a decision that they assisted in making or a decision that was made for them. The damage could already be done and new expectations will have to be established.

In simple terms, your blended family's house rules will not be exact and should not try to be the exact rules of the original family's house rules. Your blended family's house rules should be rules established by you and the biological parent to best meet the needs of you and your new blended family.

Example: As a child in your parents' home, you were taught it was okay to eat in the living areas of the home as long as you clean behind yourself. Place any paper in the garbage and any dishes are to be rinsed and placed in the dishwasher or sink immediately after the food has been consumed not after the show that may be on TV or the activity that is being performed.

This may be a house rule that you have continued without pressure because it probably became a habit in your living as an adult. Then you may expect this behavior from everyone that is living in your home.

Now you are blending a family and the chosen parents' house rule was completely opposite – no food or eating is permitted in the living room, only eat in the kitchen at the table or the bar. This rule may have been one from his or her childhood and was continued as habit into their adulthood.

So you think this is not a big deal. You are correct in one way and not as correct in the other. Suppose that the new children are not in the habit of eating meals in the living room, and you have made dinner and gone into the living room to eat expecting the stepchildren to follow your lead without invitation or permission. They take a seat at the table in the kitchen to eat instead. They may think you do not want to eat with them or you might think, "What is wrong with those kids. They don't want to eat in here in front of the television with me?" House rules are essential to establish understanding and avoidance of confusion when setting up house.

Establishing a clearly defined set of house rules might make it easier for your children, spouse, friends and family member to align their behavior with your expectations. That goes without really saying. You may not, however, be aware that having a clear set of house rules also may make it easier for assigning chores, discipline and recognizing the areas of opportunity that need improvement.

House rules should be easy-to-remember rules, and the rules should be as positive as possible. You may even consider the children assisting in making some of the rules. This act alone may demonstrate to the children that they are an important part of the family.   Kind of like when you allow children to help prepare something in the kitchen with you. Here are a few examples:

- Instead of "No loud talking or screaming in the house," try "Use your inside voice in the house."

- Instead of "Do not mess with other people's stuff," try "Respect others' belongings."
- Instead of "Do not call each other names," try "Use only each other's given or nicknames when addressing each other."
- Instead of" Do not say ugly words to each other," try "If you have no good words to say then remain silent."
- Instead of saying, "Get out of my room," try "Is there something I can do for you and remember to respect my space just as I will respect yours."

If the other home or the X-factor's house has different rules, understand that the children may try to test their boundaries. If you expect it, then you will be in a better position to already have a plan in mind and in place to counter this behavior. Simply remind them that they are at your home. You may even consider taking them outside to look at the house so they can actually see where they are located. I did this once and I never had to repeat it again.

FACT 14:   Set up your stepchildren and your family up for success not failure!

 **[Art's 20-20 Hindsight: Pounds to Ounces]**

One day after deciding I didn't want to give Jay a pound (the touching of the fist from one person to another like a high five greeting), I came up with my new concept – *the ounce*. My ounce for her was index fingertip to index fingertip instead of fist to fist. I thought was a little more personal, and it didn't have the "way to go bro" air to it.

When I saw the wow expression on my kids' faces when I gave Jay an ounce, I felt it would be good to extend it to them since I had a few ounces left over. I assigned a different finger to each of them. Jay was the index finger but I let the kids come up with their own. My daughter's ounce was hooking our pinky fingers. My son's ounce was connecting the thumbs with closed fingers as in a fist with the thumbs extended so I guess it was really an ounce and a half.

This was our personal and private high fives – the Ounce. We have been using it ever since, and the look of our special connection still peaks through on the faces. This gave each of the people in my life something shared that was unique to each individual. The ounces seem to surely add up.

 **[20-20: End]**

Did you know?

- If you are the father of children born before 1 December 2003 and you have not married their mother, you do not automatically have parental responsibility for them. This means you do not have the right to be consulted for big decisions concerning their lives, such as caring for them if the mother dies or making decisions about medical treatment. Fathers in this position can either make an agreement with the mother or apply to court for an order if she refuses to agree. Fathers who are named on the birth certificates of children born after that date will automatically have parental responsibility.

- When the stepparent acts instead of the biological parent, he or she may be denied rights that a biological parent has; for example, medical treatment. If the stepparents do not have a medical document release form stating that they are allowed to authorize treatment for the minor child, then they will be denied. This form can be obtained by an attorney who will prepare the form or notarize the form and then have both the custodial parent and the non-custodial parent, when able, to sign. When authorization is needed for schools or school related functions and other times when a stepparent wants or needs authorization, a similar document can be used. It is important that a stepparent's role in a child's life be clearly written for his or her protection.

  http://www.lawfirms.com/resources/family/marriage-and-prenuptials/stepparents-family-laws.htm

- The laws that protected United States families in the past do not provide adequate protection to members of our stepfamilies today.

  http://www.stepfamilies.info/key-advocacy-issues.php

Safeguard yourself Stepparent

Why do you need to protect yourself? Because there is very limited protection for you as a stepparent. Your life, freedom, wealth, health, and care are important.

Cohabiting Adults

If you and your partner are living in the same residence, consider drafting up a rental lease among yourselves to prevent the appearance of additional income from the X factor. Have it notarized to ensure the legality.

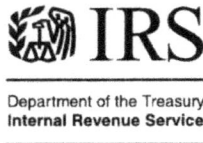

Income Tax

If the co-parent or spouse has granted you permission to file stepchildren on your taxes, obtain a written authorization from the biological parent just in case of audit or selected amnesia of the biological parent

Providing transportation

If the co-parent or spouse has granted you permission to pick up and/or drop off stepchildren to locations i.e., school, mall, friend's home, family or to or from the other biological parent location pick up obtain a written dated document allowing you authorization to avoid being falsely accused of kidnapping

Name Change

Why subtract the biological parent's last name when you can consider adding your last name in hyphenation. Check with laws of your state for name change requirements

In case of sick or injury and medical care is needed, medical care places cannot render care until a parent and/or legal guardian has been given authorization for care to be given. Obtain an authorization from the biological parent. The time waiting or time in care can make a difference.

Medical Authorization Form

I, _____, being the parent and/or legal Guardian of _____ (hereinafter, my child(ren)) Do hereby authorize _____ to seek and obtain medical care for my child(ren) in the event that my child(ren) need(s) medical care.

My child has the following allergies: _____. (if applicable)

I agree to be financially responsible for the cost of any medical care provided to my child(ren) under this Authorization. My health insurance carrier is _____ and my

Policy or Certificate number is _____. Date _____

Signature of Parent (or Legal Guardian) _____

Notary

_____

===

Travel Authorization

I, _____, being the parent and/or legal

Guardian of _____ (hereinafter, my child(ren)

do hereby authorize _____ transport in his or her chosen median of transportation for purpose of business, pleasure or recreation.

Date _____

Signature of Parent (or Legal Guardian) _____

Witness Signature._____

Notary seal

*(Most banks will notarize documents if you have an account, if not the fee is much less than any legal proceeding.)

_____

===

IRS

I, _____, being the parent and/or legal guardian of _____ (hereinafter, my child(ren) do hereby authorize _____ to claim the names of the children listed below on his or her federal income tax. He or she has provided financial care etc. for my child or children. I will not nor will the other biological parent claim the said names listed below year _____

Signature of Parent (or Legal Guardian) _____

Witness Signature._____

Notary

_____

Developing a Blended Family

On an average the living spaces for stepchildren will include a minimum of two different address locations. In an ideal world, it would be great if both homes could be managed identically, but that would be in an IDEAL world. In our real world case, it was me who decided that Art and the children have some one-on-one time in addition to time shared with the 4 of us. This decision was a win-win for me. At the time, I really did not care if it was a win-win for them. Why? Well, keep reading and you will see.

Initially, I would join Art when picking up and dropping off the children. Sometimes, this was convenient since our children lived in a different city from us, and sometimes we could have a different agenda so picking them up together would allow us to continue living our lives and include them.

I decided to stop joining him on these trips because I refused to watch him be disrespected by words or behavior from the X factor. I could not continue to take the high road or wear my "I will not drop to her level" hat. I was convinced it was best for everyone involved, especially the children, that I did not be party to this behavior. That made his picking up and dropping off a win-win for all of us.

It was during these times that our developed strategy was just conversation and not actions. It was like planning on going to a show, getting dressed making sure everything is in order at the home, work and play right down to purchasing the tickets, then at the last minute deciding not to go for no valid reason at all.

Art and I would discuss the plans, the house rules and strategies. We had a meeting of the minds of what we were ready to put into actions. Then the time would come to execute and I was the only one remembering the plan.

Art would allow himself to deviate based on the wants (not needs) of the children believing that this was the best way. If the children told him the drama they were facing in the household of their mother during these solo pickups, then he would give our plan a U-turn. That is when the cars crashed because there was no communication from him to me that the plans had changed or why the plans changed; nor was there a meeting of the minds to come up with a new workable plan.

[Art's 20-20 Hindsight: Model Relationship for the Children]

In addition to my personal vows, I wanted to show my children what a normal, successful and happy relationship would look like and that a relationship/marriage can last.

I didn't want them to think that divorce is an easy option to a disagreement. It was my goal to meet someone that I could have a loving and compassionate relationship with which would give my children another model of a relationship that they could consider normal. I wanted them to strive to achieve the same. I wanted them to see how a woman who truly cared for, loved and respected me behaves toward me. I wanted them to see that if a woman loves me, she will try to uplift me, she will naturally do things for me to make me happy, and she will get angry if someone talks against me. She will want good things to happen for me and when things were not so good she would make the best of it and stand with me during the test. She would share in my joys, and I would do the same and more for her.

I wanted us to be the role model for them. I knew I had enough love for them and someone else who wanted to be loved like I desired. I wanted to take back what I lost or thought I lost from my divorced childhood, divorced adulthood and to pave the way for my children's thinking for themselves.

[20-20: End]

FACT 15:   The biological parent of the stepchildren can only run one household and that is the one in which he or she is residing. The home of the X is just that – the home of the X with the children.

FACT 16:   Accepting FACT 15 and recognizing when and where to draw the line is as simple as locating the threshold where issues occur.

For example: The phone is always ringing at 6:00 in the morning from the X who is just talking about instances of misbehavior or lost items that cannot be found in her home.

This is not an issue that you and the stepparent should have to handle, and if your involvement is required, it does not have to be at an hour of inconvenience or inconsideration of you and your new household. Married and cohabitating couples have the resourcefulness to handle their problems at any time that works for them: however, once you have divorced your partner, you are no longer allowed the right to choose when you want married behavior such as interrupting sleep hours, ungodly before day hours and after 9 p.m. hours.

Consider this point, when cohabitating parents, married couples and non-cohabitating parents make the decision to get divorced, the relationship is no longer a social relationship. It then becomes a business deal. The decision to split time of visitation, who gets what, who lives where, all of these and more are made. Do you really think the legal system is looking at divorced couples as lost love and feel sorry for them? I do not. I believe it is strictly business.

Therefore, if the relationship has taken on a business relationship then all matters and concerns should be handled under standard business etiquette. We had to take this tone in order to save our relationship. We have listed a few problems and possible solutions for your review below:

Problem: Calling at ungodly hours for non-emergency issues with the kids

Solution: Call during assigned hours i.e., after 9:00 a.m. and before 7:00 p.m.

(If you can't take calls during these hours, have a voice box set up for messages and a method to send return messages – maybe email)

Problem: The children are not completing chores in House A.

Solution: Inform the parent that she or he needs to find a motivation to help the child learn to complete the chores or discuss with child why incompletion is the result. In other words, handle it! Just like you and the stepparent will have to handle the situation in House B.

Problem: Parent A is continually calling the children on cell phone or home phone to discuss incomplete tasks, assignments or just trying to see what they are doing at the time they are in your custody.

If the courts did not take your parental rights away and you legally have custodial rights, then exercise your rights and manage your children without the interruptions from I Spy.

Solution: Step One - Ask the X to stop calling. If X fails to comply with request, then remove the children's cell phone and/or allow calls to go to voice mail then check the message on speaker. If follow up is required, then do so; if not, disregard the problem until the children are back in the X custody.

Problem: Reporting your every move or plans to your X just to make sure if some type of emergency happens with the children you can be contacted.

Solution: Provide an emergency only contact number for your X to leave a voice message, text or email. If the issue is important enough, the X will leave a message. If this is abused, then exercise Solution II

Solution II: Selected a dedicated family member, friend, or someone in your social circle to be point of contact; then you are to be contacted by them.

These types of situations could place your kids and their stepparent in an uncomfortable situation that can and should be avoided.

Problem: Repeated fake emergency or bogus emergency calls

Solution: Tell X not to call me unless he or she is at the hospital with the child.

Get a second opinion. Talk to the child. Hopefully the child will consider you just as much his or her parent as he or she does the X.

We were in our early dating stages after meeting the children and everybody including the X. She was well aware that his past was behind him and we were taking steps forward into our relationship.

Art was under the impression by his divorce decree that he was supposed to keep his X informed of his whereabouts just in case of emergency. At that time, my employment required me to travel out of state a lot and for extended periods.

This was a great opportunity for us to see new places together. Well, that was my plan, but it was interrupted for at least seven to ten months straight. It was without fail as soon as we arrived in a new state whether it was by car or plane Art would get a phone call from his X and that, of course you guessed it, was another false emergency relating the children.

A bird's eye view into our past: I was in a state away from our home state. I had picked Art up from the airport, and we were eating in a restaurant. It was snowing outside at least four inches accumulated, and you guessed it - his phone rang, and on the other end was his X with yet another false emergency. She told him that his son had been missing for hours and could not be located. After many phone calls to friends, neighbors, the school, the hospital, and the airport, we learned that the missing child was at band practice and the X was at the hair salon. Relief? Yes! Frustrated? Yes! Ready to throw the towel in? YES! The cold that was being provided outside by the snow did not come close to the chill that was brewing on my insides.

As a woman, (the new potential stepparent) in this relationship, I was getting very frustrated with all of the drama, interruptions and created emergencies, but understood the need to respond and the need to know that everything was all right with the children. However, at this point I was convinced that all of my understanding was being misunderstood.

I just could not see how he could not see all the games that were being played on him under the umbrella "You are the father and I know you want to be a part of their lives." (IOW) I know what strings to pull in order to pull you away from anything not related to me or the children."

> Yes, we survived this bad behavior

This was a major break-it or make-it for us. This problem had to be repaired quickly or our relationship would not survive. It was at this point we began to take the time to really understand what his rights were as a parent. That's right, fathers – you have rights, so learn them; then exercise them.

We also decided that something that was simply stated in the divorce decree "letting the children know his whereabouts at all times" did not have to be that elementary. I brought it to Art's attention that she was not telling him every time she left the state, had a date or even went on a trip. He agreed and confirmed that was correct saying, "I would not know where she has taken my children or who she has around them if the children did not tell me."

Developing a blended family will require both adults to be flexible, understanding and strong in convictions, supportive, demanding and respectful while still loving each other. The definition of the word *develop* is to grow and become more mature, advanced, or elaborate.

This definition of develop is the exact act you are trying to implement. It tells you that movement, change and work will be required in developing a successful blended family, a unique but an unnatural evolution.

It is like having a lemon, a peach and water. 2 different fruits: one is bitter and the other is sweet, plus a liquid that is a necessity for life. A lemon will never become a peach, or a peach a lemon. A peach or lemon will never become water. Now the peach and the lemon can go to a liquid state with help, but they will not become water. Water will never become a piece of fruit. However, you can combine the fruits and the water to make peach lemonade, a topping for salad or even a marinade.

Developing your blended family may be work, but you can enjoy your work.

The Beginning

[Art's 20-20 Hindsight: First Introduction]

I really did not give any thought to how I felt when I was a child and my mother, who had been divorced from my father, had a guest coming over for dinner to meet us. I remember being excited because I felt the more; the merrier, and I appreciated someone who would care for my mother. After all, she was a good person, a good mother, and a hard working person. She deserved a good, intelligent person who could make the sun shine for her. I was not looking for another father, but I would be happy for her to have a good companion. After all, I might get a little fun and excitement out of the deal as well as maybe some good advice and manly know-how.

When I first invited Jay over for dinner to meet my children, I really didn't have any expectations except that I thought my children would be glad and excited to meet her. She has a warm exciting disposition. I felt like my kids had good personalities so I didn't go through the "normal preparation" with them. I just told them I had a guest coming over for dinner, and I wanted them to meet her. I felt everyone was a good fit, and this would be a formal start to building our memories and future.

Jay had asked me to make sure that I tell the kids that I was having a guest to visit me. This was to make clear that she was my guest not their guest. She was coming to see me; they just happened to be a part of the crowd had no choice in the matter.

I did not think my kids would have the same or even similar thoughts as I did when I was a child when they met Jay. I assumed that they would play it by ear in their reserved way as in being responsive and respectful to the introduction until they got to know her a little. Afterwards, they would open up a little and invite her into their world where she could also get to know them once they saw all that she had to offer us.

It was at this point where things went differently. My son was accepting and open to meeting Ms. Jay. My daughter had a different frame of mind. She was not too happy with someone she perceived as coming between her and me. She was not happy about the thought of our time being divided. She wanted what most kids wanted: mommy and daddy to be together in the same place.

After I introduced them to Ms. Jay and informed them that Ms. Jay was very special to me, I am not sure when or how it happened but their mother recognized the significance of Ms. Jay. It became clearer to me that they, the children, were getting negative feedback and static while at home from their mother, who had a tendency to say less than positive things about me and anyone I may have been involved with.

My daughter was more of a challenge for Ms. Jay than my son. She was under the impression that if she did not like Ms. Jay then she would tell her brother not to like Ms. Jay. Consequently, I would no longer like Ms. Jay.

Hold on! Change is coming. Jay had made it clear to my daughter within a short time that this was not her show and she would need to get in line. Ms. Jay was astute enough to share with me that my daughter was having some adjustment issues, and they needed some attention from me now or they would certainly get out of control.

Ms. Jay made me aware that even if she was not the next parent or woman for permanent tenure, that my daughter needed to be adjusted to her place in the pecking order which was I am her first and best man and she would always be my number 1 daughter but not my number 1 lady.

Jay was clearly ahead in the line, and I made sure that it was understood. My daughter's attitude began to slowly adjust appropriately. It was important that my children understood that I loved them then and I would always love them. Their mom and I made the decision to get divorced. It was not their fault for our decision, and they would not be part of my decision-making for my next partner. They would, however, be respectful to whomever I chose to have in my company and my life. I was hopeful as I previously stated that the woman I chose would love me and my children.

At first, I felt out of control because I wanted this new relationship to work well. I thought my children would be glad to see me happy and then understand that because I am happy, they in turn would be happier. Then I had the basic awakening: they are children—in mind, thoughts and body. I had to take the control back into my hands, get into the driver's seat, start my engine, SHIFT gears and move on toward achieving one of my ultimate goal: successfully blending my family.

I recognized in reflection that our children witnessed control or lack of control or happiness or lack of happiness in our (their mother and me) marriage. It was at our weakest points that they saw an opportunity and tried to work their way into the driver's seat. NO License to drive, then no driving shall be permitted.

 **[20-20: End]**

If you do not know the answer to something, a good place to start might be the beginning; then you may be able to work your way through the process in steps, by modeling, duplicating and simulating.

If you know the answer to a problem in mathematics, you may be able to start with it and work backwards. For example: if you had the number 4 as the solution and given number 0, 1,2,3,4 and you are asked what sum of numbers equal four, you start with what was known then you use each given factor added to another factor to add up to four. See Below. Read each equation out loud.

$$4=0+4 \quad 4=1+3 \qquad 4=2+2 \quad 4=3+1$$

The person that steps into the step parenting role is aware that he or she did not birth these children, they are not the first mother or father of these children and they recognize that the parents love their children and desire to bring their children, themselves and the new chosen mate together as a blended family.

The stepparent probably or hopefully has the best intention of loving, nurturing and guiding the children into their blended family (that is the given). The problems do not start until you have to deal with the unknown factors and the reality of expectations "I did not know it would be this hard" factor.

In the book of Genesis of the Holy Bible, there is a story about a man named Abraham who had a wife Sarah. This man was given the name "Father" years before he became a daddy. His wife Sarah was barren (she had not borne any children within the 10 years granted to bear a child). This was a stigma against her. God had told Abraham that he would be the father of many nations and his wife overheard God telling this to Abraham. He believed what God had told him and entered into agreement.

In the story, God told him the plan, but He did not give him or Sarah any dates, timelines, hints about when this great covenant would be a reality. Time was moving in years for Abraham and his wife. It was now past the baby-making season for his wife. Things were not looking too good at this point.

So, Abraham asked God how was this to be so if he had not children of his seed. He was given an orphan male child and he took this child in his employment and his heart, but God informed him that this slave child was not his heir.

Abraham and Sarah took matters into their own hands and decided that her slave Hagar, a gift from Sarah's homeland king, would be a surrogate mother for her and her husband. That way, Abraham would have an heir so the prophecy would be come true.

It was a good plan in Sarah's mind. Abraham agreed to mate with the slave, and they produced a son. This made Abraham, the father, and Sarah, the first stepmom recorded in the Bible, and Hagar, the biological mother, become a blended family.

All was well until jealousy and insecurity of her misfortune of being barren and the joy of the child crept into the plan. Before the pregnancy was completely termed, the story will speak of a conflict between Sarah and the slave mistress Hagar. The story says the wife went to the husband complaining of it, and he told her to handle it. Her handling of the situation eventually led to the fleeing of the pregnant slave mistress Hagar.

On her runaway journey, an angel came to Hagar and asked her a couple of questions; then told her to go back and have her son. He would be the prince of many nations. She was obedient.

The son was born and for twelve to thirteen years the son was the only child; then in the elderly age of Sarah and Abraham, God blessed them with their own bloodline son. This caused conflict from what I believe Sarah's misunderstanding.

Sarah was being mocked by the people of the land for having a baby so late in her years and she witnessed Hagar and her son laughing together. (This is a normal action between mothers and children laughing together). Sarah also did not want to share the legacy promised to the first-born son. So Sarah once again went to her husband telling him that the slave and the child must go and they will not be part of her son's inheritance.

Now Abraham, being a man titled "Father", informed his wife that the slave's son was his son, also. After standing fast in conviction, Abraham received word from God to send the slave and the child away. He was also informed of the good fortune. The child would be protected and promised a good future because he was recognized by God to be Abraham's son.

In the synopsis of this story, I interjected my personal revelation in order to allow you to make your own decision about this story. We have included a copy of this text in the index under Bible Text and Stories.

The story above was shared to demonstrate the role of the first wife's interference, jealousy, insecurity and lack of responsibility to accept the responsibility of decision-making in which she took an active role and how it impacted the blended family. As a matter of fact, it was her idea to rush the plans of God and try to save face in her old age. Have you noticed any of these behaviors in your X?

- X Factor goes to co parent complaining about stepparent or the role of the stepparent

- X husband or wife listen but does not act
- Stepparent leaves (physically and or mentally)
- Stepparent may return to die another day or not return at all

In my opinion, the story demonstrates that the father was willing to accept his responsibility and acknowledge his child, but he did not stop the confusion created by his wife in the beginning. When the rubber hit the highway and she had her own child, she kicked up the drama a notch. Why could she not have just recognized the blessing of her new baby having a big brother and her child having two moms (herself and a stepmom) and she would be two moms, (mom to her child and stepmom)? After almost missing her chance to have any children, now she would be the parent and stepparent of two children. It is also a story of stepchildren who have the opportunity of having multiple parents.

If the co-parent of the stepchildren decides to straddle the fence because he or she seems to be caught in the middle of the past family and the future family, it may place them in a good observation position and not the best position for participation. Both observation and participation are good acts; however, the results of each will be different. Observation alone will allow results to be seen and participation will assist in making results happen.

The story demonstrated the slave did not have a choice in deciding who would be the father of her child, her role, her staying or going from their home; her abuse or her misuse were not options to her. She was a slave so the options were not available to her although she was being used to be the answer to the promise from God. Hagar, however, for her child, was obedient. Just as the stepparent did not have a choice of its stepchildren. We are not implying that the stepparent is a slave nor be treated as a slave: "Do as I say, when I say it" and not have opinions about what is being said or done.

Let's take a closer look at the end results of this story without all of the details.

- Abraham's marriage to Sarah
- Abraham's mates with Hagar
- Mating with Hagar yielded the a son first son named Ishmael
- Sarah and Hagar conflict
- Conflict resolution
- Abraham mates with wife Sarah and a second son named Isaac
- Hagar and Sarah conflict

- Wife requests servant and her child be dismissed
- Abraham grieves over decision both are his sons
- Abraham gets a word from God
- Abraham sends Hagar and child away
- Abraham and Hagar are separated
- Hagar is now single mom with child -- a package deal
- Second mating partner severed because of the X Factor.

Did you know that the divorce rate has been reported as high as 74% for second marriages? That means only about 26% of second marriages survive. In other words, for every 100 second marriages, only 26 out of the 100 will survive.

That would imply that if the parent with the "package deal" was to remarry that this family will only have a 26% chance of survival. If you were to list the third marriage ratios of failure and success, applause could be requested for second marriages' statistics.

Why is the divorce rate so high in second marriages? According to statistics second-marriage-failure rate is so high because of:

- marital problems
- parenting differences
- the X factor
- overwhelming challenges of step parenting
- under appreciation of stepparent
- lack of communication
- the complicated emotions of the children
- the parent and the stepparent relationship not being able to handle the drama
- the co-parent not championing for the stepparent
- the co-parent not enforcing their house rules
- the step parenting not being able to completely parent
- lack of control
- lack of power to stand up for the new blended family
- the lack of ability to stop looking back
- the inability to continue to look forward
- self-esteem
- self-doubt
- standards and/or lack of set standards

↓ negative, external influences

This list is not absolute. There are many more reasons, but the ones listed were most prevalent in our steps taken to take the step out of step parenting.

We recognized that there is no right way to be a stepparent. We repeat - there is not a right way to be a stepparent. There are many bad, ugly ways to be a stepparent. We will not focus on the latter in this book.

Society seemingly holds the stepparent to a higher standard of expectations. Listed are the two major ones—barely allowing room for exception to its rules:

1. Society practically demands unconditional love toward the stepchildren regardless of behavior,

2. Society expects the stepparent to respect invisible boundaries and feelings of the stepchildren, the biological father or mother, the X-factor and former in laws, all without so much as having one law to protect the stepparent or officiate the boxing matches that could occur.

This glass ceiling of societal standards can easily lead to self-doubt, low self-esteem, re-thinking of one's relationship, loneliness, hopelessness, fear, depression, betrayal, and defeat, thus allowing one to take on the title "Detached Stepparent."

You're okay for feeling any and all of these emotions; however, we are encouraged that this book will provide you with a stable foundation to build the home and lives of your blended family. Even if your blended family is not brand new and if you allow yourself the flexibility to accept the suggested changes and implement them in your blended family, success will be closer in proximity than failure.

Remember, blended families will have concerns that are exclusive to blended families. Yes, it is true. Your issues will not be the same as a traditional family with children. So if you get into the comparison game, try to make sure you are matching an apple with an apple and a lemon with a lemon.

Step in Front of Your Stepparent

Taking a "step in front of your stepparent" is the most important step you will take after you have assumed or have decided you will be in the relationship with this person who will become the stepparent to your children. This step should be figuratively, but let's not discard physically, depending on your situation.

To say "there's never a dull moment when blending two families" is an understatement. Listed below are some of the common issues. In our research and experiences, we agree with many child and family psychologists who say blended families are challenging. The list below is just the tip of the iceberg of issues that may be encountered as a stepparent:

1. Understanding the changes
2. Accepting the change
3. Kid/stepparent conflicts
4. Sibling jealousy
5. Bonding issues
6. Problems with the X Factor
7. Insecurity in the kids
8. Competition for parental affection
9. Favoritism (or the appearance of)
10. Out-of-control kids
11. Guilt and parental guilty behavior
12. Expectations
13. Time
14. Money
15. Respect or lack of respect
16. Appreciation

Many stepparents, who do not consider the dynamics of the household before they marry or join the blended family they love, may find themselves faced with some of issues mentioned above. The stepparent may not have a clear understanding of the role that the parent of the children is expecting of them in this blended family.

What are you saying, Jay? If I am to be the stepmom, I will take on the role of the mother in our household. If I am to be the stepdad, then I will take on the role of the dad.

It may look that simple, but the reality is that it is not that simple or cut and dry. There are many gray areas that need to be covered which should happen before permanent black and white situations are set up.

These types of dynamics exist because the woman or man you love has let it evolve into what it is. Their normal situation may include rude or unruly behavior, no structure, out of control or "this is to be expected" behavior from the children. In a nutshell, the children do what they know the parent will allow them to do. The household aspects for the children will only change when the adults (both step and biological) have the desired willingness to change it and support it.

A new stepdad or stepmom is not in a great position in this situation. If the stepparent tries to force the children to change their behavior, the children may resist or decide that the stepparent is the enemy.

The custodial mom or custodial dad has to play the "bad guy" in this case, and the stepparent will have to play a supporting role. Both adults will also have to make the changes gradually. Children do not like change. If you are aware that your child does not like medicine even if it will make them feel better, do you decide not to give them the medicine? Heck no! Now that I think about it, many adults do not like change even if they demanded the change to occur. Perhaps there should be a class on "How to accept change in style?"

Suggested steps to take to step in front of your stepparent:

1. Speak with your mate about your role, their expectations, parenting styles in general and how the two of you are going to handle discipline.
2. Agree to disagree then come to a workable solution.
3. Agree to the specifics of the solution, understand the agreement and stick to it them.
4. Allow time for both of you to work toward your goals.
5. Complete the companion training workbook located in the back of this book. (*A free gift for your purchase*).
6. Do not allow anyone, especially your X, your children or family, to have any negative comments in your presence or their absence. Demand respect or silence the comment.
7. It is recommended that you do not allow yourself to be involved in a negative conversation about your new partner (stepmother or stepfather) with your X.

The losing team does not generally come back with compliments on how well the winning team played. You are giving them fuel for the fire and it will come back to burn you.

8. If you are not in a position to demand respect, simply walk away from the conversation, end the phone call, make no response to the text or email or if on social media, do not entertain ignorance in a public medium. Again, you are giving them fuel for the fire and it will come back to burn you.

9. If you are receiving written comments via text, Facebook or email, then responded strongly in the writing "This will not be tolerated and terminate this behavior immediately. I will have to have the court decide if this is proper behavior as it relates to my children."

10. Respect your relationship, the feeling of the person that is in the role of stepparent, and do not (and I repeat Do Not!) fear losing the love of your children. It won't happen!

11. If you should lose whatever relationship with the X that remains after your divorce or separation, remember you are no longer in an emotional relationship with them. It is because of them or you both that you have arrived to your current situation. Keep in the forefront of your mind that you are only communicating with them because of the children and the children alone. It is a business relationship.

12. If you have unfinished business with that relationship, finish it! Read our book, <u>Deliverance "Unfinished Business"</u>, coming soon to a bookstore or e site.

13. BE "Divorced with children."

14. BE "Married with stepparent and children."

15. BE Supportive of the stepparent.

16. BE the Hero or SHERO for the stepparent.

17. Did you know that some courts accept texts and emails as legal documents?

18. Do not make it a habit of living your new life in fear or threats.

19. Put your X on notice that you will set it up so that a mediator or judge can hear his or her concerns.

20. Understand your rights as a parent of the children you are working so diligently to love.

21. Understand your divorce, separation and custodial rights to your children

Communication is the one key that will lead you both to a successful blended family. We would like to invite you and your partner to take a look at "How to Listen" information in companion *workbook located in the back of this book.*

There is a childhood fairy tale that comes to my mind to emphasize how you can ensure that your chosen stepparent is not threatened just because you had to move on from your past relationship. The story is entitled: <u>Three Little Pigs</u>. You know the one with the big bad wolf. (*In our scenario, the houses represent the blended family home and the wolf represents the X factor.*)

Once upon a time, there were three little pigs that lived with their mother in a meadow. (*Represents the Original Family- mom, dad and children*)

One day, the mother pig said to the three little pigs, "You need to go out into the world and make your own way." So they waved "goodbye" and out into the world they went. (*Divorce, Separation*)

The pigs decided to build houses near the woods. They accepted their responsibilities and recognized they could not stay at their mom's home anymore. She wanted them to move on with their lives.

Now a big bad wolf lived in the woods, and he was not happy when he saw the three little pigs building houses nearby. He was thinking, "What! They are moving on with their lives out here in my territory? Not on my watch, as long as there is breath in my lungs, they will not live without me trying to eat them." This is so perfect. (*The X Factor is not happy when the children are happy living or being with you and the stepparent.*)

The first little pig was lazy. He made a house of straw. The big bad wolf huffed and puffed and blew it down. (*Allowed abuse to stepparent - relationship ended quickly.*)

The second little pig worked a little harder than the first little pig. He made a house of twigs. The big bad wolf huffed and puffed and blew the house down. (*Some support but not enough to protect the stepparent or your relationship.*)

The third little pig made a house of bricks. The big bad wolf huffed and puffed and he huffed and puffed. He took a break because he was becoming exhausted and could not understand why this house would not go down as easily as the other two pigs' homes. He returned; then he huffed and puffed some more, but the house did not fall down. (*Did not allow abuse and stood toe to toe in supporting stepparent- relationship and blended family survived.*)

This made the big bad wolf very, very angry. He went up on the roof and tried to get into the house through the chimney. He climbed into the chimney and slid down into a pot of boiling water. He ran out of the house and never came back! (*The X Factor –this list is enumerable when the x factor recognizes he or she is losing the battle to destroy, hurt, or harm you, your relationship, and may not have any happiness themselves.*)

It is a good thing that the pig living in the brick home decided he was not going to allow his home to be destroyed by the big bad wolf like his siblings did. He considered every entrance to his home and thought of a way to protect it from entry of the big bad wolf. His thoughts were to save his home and his siblings who were now residing with him, even if it caused some hurt to the wolf.

The wolf should not have been trying to destroy his home or come in without being invited. He was not Santa Claus so he should not have even been on the roof. The end!

"Build your blended family's home out of bricks then be prepared to defend any entrance into the home." JamArt

[Art's 20-20 Hindsight: A Good Offense]

Let's talk football – the American football game. Some of us are football addicts, and others are clueless of the game. So we borrowed the verbiage from websites to describe how football relates to stepparent scenarios. (IOW) We would like to use the game of football and compare it to the real life scenario of blended family vs. X factor. Just like in football, the blended family is always trying to move forward, which would make them the offense.

One 11-man team has possession of the football. This team is called the offense. It tries to advance the ball down the field by running with the ball or passing it to score points by crossing the goal line - an area called the end zone.

The blended family team may consist of as few as 3 players including the children. This team is trying to establish itself and obtain social and economic growth and development.

The other team (also with 11 players) is called the defense. It tries to stop the offensive team and make it give up possession of the ball. If the team with the ball does score or is forced to give up possession, the offensive and defensive teams switch roles (the offensive team goes on defense and the defensive team goes on offense). This continues, back and forth, until all four quarters of the game have been played.

The X Factor team may consist of as few as 2 players, including the children, to a number that is not known if one included all of society, families, and friends, social and business relationships. This team's goal is to throw as many obstacles in the way of the blended family's goals as possible.

For simplicity sake, the blended family will always be the offense and X Factor will be the defense.

THE KEY PLAYERS

Each team has 3 separate units: the offense (see section below), those players who are on the field when the team has possession of the ball; the defense (see section below), players who line up to stop the other team's offense; and special teams that only come in on kicking situations (punts, field goals, and kickoffs). Only 11 players are on the field from each team at any one time.

The Quarterback   The Biological Parent (co-parent)

Wide Receiver/Running Back the Stepparent

THE FIELD

The field measures 100 yards long and 53 yards wide. Little white markings on the field are called yard markers, which help the players, officials, and the fans keep track of the ball. Probably the most important part of the field is the end zone. It's an additional 10 yards on each end of the field. This is where the points add up! When the offense, the team with possession of the ball, gets the ball into the opponent's end zone, they score points.

The fields for our two teams are the homes of the blended family and the home of the X factor. The getting to end zone is when the blended family has stopped the X factor from interfering, throwing obstacles or causing confusion, or at least, making the

X factor think twice about doing it. All progression in taking the step out of step parenting can be measured in the movement of the new blended family forward and or backward, toward or away from their primary goal. That is – to blend their new family successfully.

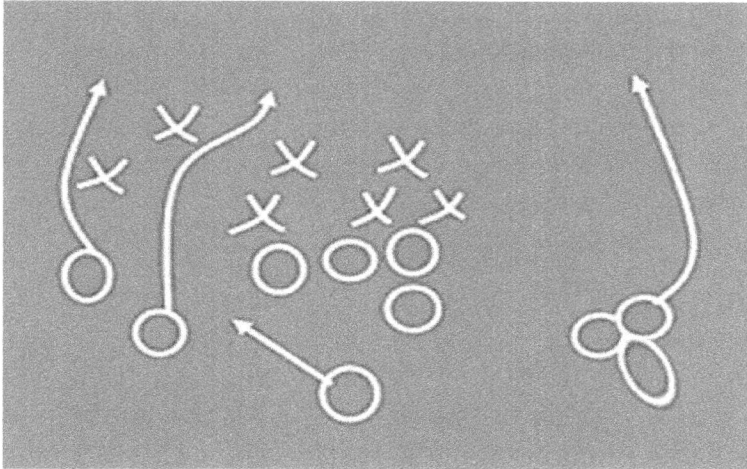

THE KICKOFF

A game starts with the kickoff. The ball is placed on a kicking tee at the defense's 30-yard line and a special kicker on the defensive team (a "placekicker") kicks the ball to the offense. A kickoff-return man from the offense will try to catch the ball and advance it by running. Where he is stopped is the point from which the offense will begin its drive or a series of offensive plays.

This games start when the X factor realizes that their X (your co-parent) has decided to move on with his or her life in a new relationship. The X factor will see that you and your co-parent (your partner) are making gains in life and love which cause the X factor to work a defensive game to stop and stall all gains using all means available including sideline coaches (friends, children and other family members).

FIRST DOWN

All progress in a football game is measured in yards. The offensive team tries to get as much "yardage" as it can to try to move closer to the opponent's end zone. Each time the offense gets the ball it has four downs or chances to gain 10 or more yards. If the offensive team successfully moves the ball 10 or more yards, it earns a first down and another set of four downs. If the offense fails to gain 10 yards, it loses possession of the ball. The defense tries to prevent the offense not only from scoring but also from gaining the 10 yards needed for a first down. If the offense reaches fourth down, it usually punts the ball (kicks it away). This forces the other team to begin its drive further down the field.

A first down happens when the X factor causes your plans or you to go south. For instance, when you and your partner are getting the children for the first time and introduction, one of the children makes an insulting statement obviously implanted by the X factor. These statements can cause confusion or ill feeling toward one or all of you. To say the least, you may have thought the children would know better, but you can't count on that. The X factor will, however. You can count on the children hearing or over hearing all sorts of negative comments whether they may or may not believe them. You have to counter these comments when they surface. Back into huddle.

MOVING THE BALL - The Run and the Pass

A play begins with the snap. At the line of scrimmage (the position on the field where the play begins) the quarterback loudly calls out a play in code and the player in front of him, the center passes or snaps the ball between his legs to the quarterback. From there, the quarterback can throw the ball, hand it off, or run with it.

A play begins the same way with a SNAP. The X Factor does something in code (the co-parent does not get a clear picture of the play being called) then the attitudes take the front and center and the confusion begins. It could be the co-parent's attitude of adjustment, the attitude of misunderstanding or the attitude of "no they are not going to be happy in a new life and think they are going to do it without the children."

THE RUN

There are two main ways for the offense to advance the ball. The first is called a run. This occurs when the quarterback hands the ball off to a running back who then tries to gain as many yards as possible by eluding defensive players. The quarterback is also allowed to run with the ball.

This play begins when you have made gains in rebuking the X factor dilemma by making it clear that things like delays when you pick up the kids, late nonemergency phone calls, calling and calling when the kids are visiting with you, appointments made on your time with the kids, etc., are not going to be tolerated. There is more, but we will save some for another play.

THE PASS

The other alternative to running the ball is to throw it or as they say in football, pass it! Usually, the quarterback does the passing though there are times when another player may pass the ball to confuse the defense. A pass is complete if another offensive player, usually the "wide receiver", catches the ball. If the ball hits the ground before someone catches it, it is called an incomplete pass.

The completed pass with yardage: this is one of those weekends where you start to see some respect from the X or they, at least, are beginning to understand that you will stand up for your stepparent's (partner) and your rights by making it clear that the X cannot talk to you or your stepparent any kind of way.

THE TACKLE

The defense prevents the offense from advancing the ball by bringing the ball carrier to the ground. A player is tackled when one or both of his knees touch the ground. The play is then over. A play also ends when a player runs out of bounds.

This is when you think you are on the way. All is great but the X slides in an insult to your stepparent (partner) via child courier. You have just arrived home with the children and one of the children says to you in front of your partner, "I heard mommy say that you have lost your taste in partners and you really grabbed one from the very bottom. Is that true?" After all of the work you have done, teaching and preaching, "Do not pass information between houses," it feels more like a fumble.

FIELD GOAL = 3 POINTS

If the offense cannot score a touchdown, it may try to kick a field goal. Field goals are worth three points and often are the deciding plays in the last seconds of close games. They can be attempted from anywhere on the field on any down, but generally are kicked from inside the defense's 45-yard line on fourth down. For a field goal to be "good," the placekicker (or field goal kicker) must kick the ball through the goal-post uprights and over the crossbar. The defense tries to block the kick and stop the ball from reaching the goal post.

Three point field goal: This is when it feels like trouble, but you have been careful enough to recover, i.e. when the X demands that you should pay more child support and takes you to court. You have been spending extra money on the children's needs while they mismanaged the child support. In court, you present not only proof of all of your on time child support payments but you have all of your receipts for all of the extras you have paid for. The courts drop the cases.

TURNOVERS

While trying to advance the football to the end zone, the offense may accidentally turn the ball over to the defense in one or two ways: a fumble or an interception.

After a great and exciting weekend with the kids, you take them home on Sunday evening. The kids are still talking about fun things they experienced. They eagerly grab their backpacks and run into the house singing and smiling. Sounds great so far, but by the time you get home, one of the children calls you saying that their mother got very angry with them for no reason, yelled at them and put them on punishment claiming that they were the worst kids ever.

WINNERS OF THE GAME

The team that plays the best game and scores the most points on the scoreboard is the winner of the game. Yes, there are other statistics recorded for each team. Some even break records but the bottom line is to learn from your losses, keeping your head in the game and playing every game like you want to win.

The winners of the blended family are measured by successfully avoiding and recovering from tackles, fumbles, and turnovers then scoring the most rewarding accomplishments and beating all the odds for you and your blended family. RAH! RAH! GO BLENDED FAMILY! GO!!!

[20-20: End]

Back to the Basics

The children are important, but they are not first in the blended family. Oops, I should not have said that. I know your children will not come behind any man or woman. "My children are my life!" Are you thinking these words?

We would like to take this moment to share a story with you from the Bible. The Bible is the Christian road map and guide to life, and I believe in it, its teachings and the lessons that we can learn from it with the right understandings, interpretations and revelations.

Genesis, Chapter 4, tells the story about Adam and Eve, first man and woman, coming together as one. Then a child was born (Cain), and a second son (Abel) was born to the couple. Adam and Eve told both of their sons about the message God had given them, and they should make a sacrifice to show how much they appreciated all God had done and to atone for their sins.

Now Abel (the youngest son) was very concerned about his sacrifice. Cain was not as dedicated to the request. A turn of events happened in the story where Cain struck Abel to the ground and killed him. Now, if you image the chaos that might have happened in the home of ADAM and EVE after learning of the death of their youngest son by the hand of their eldest son.

If you can recall an experience where you were supposed to be watching the children including a neighbor's, a family member's or friend's children and you did not meet the expectations of your spouse or the parent, the feedback from them was not a compliment. You may have seen or heard some very real but ugly emotions. For example, no snacks and you allowed the children one little piece of candy.

In this particular biblical story, I can imagine all types of questions asked from Adam to Eve and from Eve to Adam:

Adam asked, "Where were you?" "How could you let this happen?"

Eve replied, "If you were not in the garden spending time talking to God, you could have been with my baby"?

"Oh really! This is my fault. If you were not slipping around talking to the serpent in the garden, you could have been watching out for my baby," Adam responded.

I shared that story to show that the Bible gave a bird's eye view into this fact - children will bring their own drama to your relationship and it will be vital that you and your partner survive the drama and stay together. The relationship of Adam and Eve remained intact.

I believe that Adam and Eve's relationship remained intact because the Bible tells me so. I am here to assist in writing this book to show you that, yes – your children are important, but they should not be placed before your new spouse, relationship partner or significant other.

If you allow the children to be more important than your spouse, then why did you choose to accept divorce from the previous parent of the children as a solution? Why should you expect more of the new spouse or significant other?

It was not an overnight manifestation with us, but it did become our primary focal point to stay committed to our love and our strategy. The spoken commitment that we would love each more than enough, to stand together in our strategy and not allow his children, the X, naysayers or anyone to divide and dismantle our decision to make him and me an **"US"**!

In the beginning before you and your X had children, it was you and he or she, two consenting hopeful grown adults. Then after you had children; it became two adults with children.

There is a pattern here: married, cohabitating, or just friends with benefits—the adults then the children. Stay with us now. We know times have changed in every way. We are living proof, and this book is just the tip of the iceberg of what is to become the standard normal.

- Did your child ask you and your X to get a divorce so that the children can become rulers?
- Did you and your X consult your children about getting a divorce and whatever their decision was, you and your X would agree to those terms?
- Did you and your X inform your children that you were getting a divorce and then inform them that they would now take on the role as parents?

- Will you allow your children to overrule your new chosen mate?
- Will you allow children to run amok on your chosen guest?
- Will you allow your children to disrespect you, your parents, your employer, your employees, your friends, your neighbors, your pastor or even your pet?
- Are willing to allow your children to become ruler over you and your X?

- Is it acceptable for your children to be disruptive, disrespectful and totally ignore the teachers or authority figures?

The answer to the previously listed question should be NO! And some may get a H*** NO!

Tell me where and how do these statements come into play in the big scheme of family, hierarchy and structure? If you have not said these words, we are convinced that you have at least heard them.

"My children come first!"
"Nobody comes before my children!"
"I am living for my children!"
"Wait for love until after your children are grown and gone!"
"My children are the most important in my life before any man or woman!"
"I will just die for my children!"

Calm yourself. We are not saying in any way, form or fashion that your children are not important, nor are we implying that you love your children any less or more, for that matter, than any other parent, grandparent, aunt, stepparent, or guardian by moving forward into a new relationship that will hopefully be for the best for you, the children and your new partner.

The point is we would like for you to really consider what you are saying when you are asking another adult to come into your life and assist you in nourishing your greatest assets (the children) and giving you the life of love you desire.

If you say your children come first, does that mean that your mate comes second? Is this the rule only for stepparents?

Did you expect your X to suddenly change his or her role and allow your children to disrespect, call the shots, make the family decisions and determine what is best for the family after divorce? NO! NO! NO!

FACT 17:   Do not expect more from a stepparent than you would expect from your X or yourself?

FACT 18:   If you allowed your children to run your relationship and it was a failure, do not repeat this failure. The results will be the same!

The point of this conversation is children will just have to get in line behind the adults. Every organization has a structure, pecking order; so does the family.

Our job is to nourish, love and groom the children to become mature responsible adults. The child's job is not to raise the adults.

In the scenarios below, we ask you, the reader, the question, what is the best solution that would provide safety and support for the children and the adults?

There is group of four people on a raft in the middle of an ocean with an inhabitable island within site. The four people consist of man, woman and two children. In the scenarios, you are yourself and the opposite sex is your mate.

Scenario 1-2   Man swims takes one child to the island to safety then returns to the raft where a woman and child remain on the raft.

　　*This leaves a child on the island alone.

Scenario 3 -4 *Man swims takes woman to the island to safety then returns to the raft where 2 children on the raft.*

　　*This leaves an adult on the island alone

This is how this scenario can work out for the good of all involved. You see by assisting the adult to safety, she will be on the island, possibly resting up just a little. The man goes back to get one of the children, she may be able to meet him to retrieve the child and remain on the island with the child. (An adult and a child to safety.)

She may be able to exchange places with him and go get the other child. (An adult and a child to safety.) Now the man's strength has had a chance to be replenished a little. So on her return with the other child, he may be able to assist if necessary.

The 3rd & 4th scenarios represent a man and woman working together to save the children and each other.

If a child is taken to the island first and the other adult and child are left on the raft, there will be a child on the island alone. Sure there will be two children on the raft alone, but at least, they will have each other and they would be familiar with their surrounding versus being along in a new, unfamiliar island.

Now let me bring this scenario home, I used this illustration on several occasions to try to get Art to understand that if we work together, we will be able to show his children (my stepchildren) how we as parents would do our best to provide for them, keep them safe, love them and also take care of each other.

Remember, too, that "the most important relationship to nurture in any stepfamily is between the adult partners," say experts in the field. In fact, putting more energy and priority in your relationship may improve your relationships with everyone that is in direct influence of the children, who will begin to see you as a strong, united front instead of two perplexed individuals. (This may have been the behavior they witnessed from both biological parents or maybe not).

To accomplish this goal, we strongly recommend that time is planned to be alone with your partner to discuss family issues. We would also like to add that the two of you should not handle these discussions in the bed that is shared. Keep the places that you both come together as lovers, friends and soul mates free of any drama and trauma. In other words, do not practice taking your problem to bed!

At each meeting, pick the most significant problems you are facing then work toward harmonious solutions. At the end of each meeting, do something special together. You know the routine: work then play. Here are some suggestions of things to do after working together and devising strategies for blending your family successfully:

- Share a dessert, eating it from one plate (use different utensil if required).
- Give each other back rubs or massages while listening to your favorite music like the cd "Tribute to Greatness" by vocalist Lutalo "SweetLu Olutosin" (www.sweetlumusic.com)
- Watch a movie sitting or lying together. That's right, bodies touching.

- Share a cold or hot drink and discuss your favorite times shared or plan your next great time together. No talk about children is permitted. ☺
- Make a special dessert or meal together in the kitchen intentionally bumping into each other, giving kisses or delivering a love tap in special places while you work. Use your best dinnerware. If you get carried away in the moment, make sure all appliances are turned off.
- Discuss starting a business together that could bring in a residual income (for your annual family's support), for example a savings plan in gold like Karatbars. It is working for us. www.americasgoldclub.com
- All of the energy put into planning, scheduling, and communicating will be rewardingly justified in itself. So, we strongly encourage celebrating the "U" in us. That is – you both are coming together as 2 separate people to become one unified couple
- Together negate the goal of the children and the X, which can divide you from your loved one. Don't become the ultimate Ice Cream Daddy, Ready Made Babysitter, Handyman of Convenience, and don't be the one left alone when their schedules are too busy for you to be a part.

You deserve to be happy; the new chosen stepparent deserves to be able to enjoy you and the family that came with you devoid of your X's interference or fragments of maladjustments.

As for Art and me, we cannot move forward without telling you about how often we had to fall down. That's right! Fall down on our knees to pray for some help, guidance and some "how do we get past this one this time" and "what else is next."

We fell down a lot, but we are thankful that we not did fail. We were thankful that when we did fall down, both of us did not fall prey at the same time, and we allowed the other one to help the other up.

It was not easy for me being in this relationship in the stepparent role. I will say with no reservation that Art eventually recognized the hardship of my role. He began to sense my emotional involvement as stepparent and learned what burden and responsibility the title carried. I had assumed the role to assist in achieving his goal for his children and himself. Now, he made my role as his woman a gift that I do cherish.

We found going *Back to the Basics* to be most influential in our growth. We just started with the alphabets creating the list below as a daily reminder commitment to making our blended family successful: (Come on, don't you remember "abcdefg hijk lmnop qrs tuv wxy and z. Now, I said my ABCs, wontcha come and play with me.")

(A)   Attitude

(B)   Behavior

(C)   Communications and control

(D)   Destroy the demons

(E)   Expect the unexpected

(F)   Find workable solutions

(G)   Guard your ultimate goals

(H)   Help each other pass OVER the rough spots

(I)   Important before Injustice

(J)   Jump behind each in support

(K)   Knowledge

(L)   Love

(M)   Mission

(N)   NO and NOT acceptable

(O)   Opposed our haters

(P)   Proactive planning

(Q)   Quit living in fear

(R)   Respect was not a request

(S)   Set standards

(T)   Together we stood

(U)   Unified our purpose

(V)   Victory was our prayer

(W)   Winning was our only option

(X)   EX understood

(Y)   WHY he or she was not in control of our lives

(Z)   *"Zip out the bad behavior and Zip up the good" jrn*

We welcome the opportunity for you to introduce, practice and help this list to grow with back-to-the-basic practices to assist in this important behind-the-scene role of step parenting and co-parenting. Email suggestions to takingthestepoutlw@gmail.com

"Perfect Practice makes Perfection" jrn

The Heart of the Fruit

KJV Luke 6:45 A good man out of the good treasure of his heart bringeth forth that which is good; and an evil man out of the evil treasure of his heart bringeth forth that which is evil: for of the abundance of the heart his mouth speaketh.

A rollover tradition with Art and his daughter continued in our home. The two of them shared time in the kitchen creating some type of food delight. This was a tradition that I supported with eagerness believing that it was important that she and her brother spend time alone with their father doing things or not doing anything. So without fail for the first few months of our blended family, they would make this grand fruit salad that would include a variety of fresh fruits.

Fruit salad is a dish consisting of various kinds of fruit, sometimes served in a liquid either in their own juices or syrup. When served as an appetizer or as a dessert, a fruit salad is sometimes known as fruit cocktail or a fruit cup.

Our daughter was having a difficult time transitioning from being divorced from her father and their living in separate homes. She did not understanding the belittling words about her dad and me from her mother and that her father could and was loving someone differently than he was loving her, her brother, and the way he did not love their mother.

I noticed this behavior not sure her father was aware at the time. Art asked me one day how was I going to get her to change her attitude and help her blend into the family we were cultivating. My response was not one you would expect after reading this book, but I told him, "I am not going to do anything. I do not need her to love you, nor do I need her to love your son. If she chooses to remain a stick in the mud, then let her sink like quicksand."

I also told him, "I am doing everything I know humanly possible to relate to her, but you need to understand she is receiving directives from her mother or someone else. She has taken it upon herself to champion whatever their mission is and I am not getting dressed for that party, nor will I be participating. We will go on, enjoy our lives, and if decides she wants to be a part then maybe if I am in the receiving mood, we will move from blended of three to a blended family of four."

That is right. I let it be known that I had a choice in this matter. I could be a great stepmom or I could be a not-so-great stepparent. I did not sign up for fighting demons and dealing with the bad attitude of Art's daughter. I would not tolerate her bad behavior and she would respect me, but she did not now or ever have to love me.

I was not trying to be her mother. That position had been taken, and she would always be her mother's daughter. You all may believe I signed up for a package deal. Wrong! My agreement was with Art. His children were optional for me. They had a living mom and dad. No vacancy was available for a parent. However, stepparent was an option if both parties were willing.

Well, I have purchased packages of items before and returned them, but I paid for them. I did not ask for her to be here, nor did I choose to have her in this type of relationship; so I am not paying. If anyone was to pay, it was to be the two of them that made her. This was my take after months and more months of efforts.

Sometimes during the stages of learning to stand, crawl or walk, you just have to make sure the perimeter is safe and let the child try to find its own understanding allowing it to stand, crawl; and subsequently, it will walk. I felt that this would be the best way to help my stepdaughter come around.

Shortly thereafter Art asked me to take my stepdaughter to the grocery store to pick up some fruit for the fruit salad. I did not want to do it. I thought it would be great if he, my stepson and stepdaughter took the journey. It would be their time alone without me, some time together for them, and I would get some time alone without the children. I really never desired to spend any time away from Art, but I was willing to take one for the team.

I am a team player, so I really did take one for the team and agreed to drive her to the store. This ride turned out to be an opportunity for God to give me a revelation and to give her an understanding that her heart was larger than she was allowing it to be.

We were in the car, no words being spoken, just the universal language - music playing on the CD player. The thought came in to my head "What is up with this little girl?" So the next thing you know, I am speaking these words out of my mouth, "So missy … what is really going on with you?"

She said, "What are you talking about?"

I repeated the question then I added, "You come over to OUR house, arriving with a bad attitude on Friday, then you level out on Saturday, then back to the funky you by the time it is for you to return to your mother's home?"

She remained silent just looking at me as if I just looked into a crystal ball and read her fortune. We arrived at the grocery store and went inside to get the fruit. She got the basket and began putting various fruits in the basket: apples, oranges, honeydew melon, cantaloupe, watermelon, grapes, pears, peaches and bananas. I asked her, "Do you wish to get all of this fruit?"

She responded, "Yes."

This is when the Divine Intervention began. I was clueless and I did not have a road map so I became obedient. I asked her, "Do you like all these fruits?"

"I love all of this fruit!" She responded with a corrective tone.

I picked up the bag of apples and asked her, "If I remove the bag of apples, would you like bananas any less?"

She responded, "NO."

I then picked up the watermelon and asked, "If I remove the watermelon from the cart, would you love or like cantaloupe any less?"

She responded, "NO".

I said "NO, what?"

She said "No, Ma'am." I repeated this procedure about 5 times with different fruits and each time she said no if one were removed she would not like or love any of the other fruit any less. By the time we repeated the steps a couple times, she was laughing and I was asking her questions like are you sure? Really?

I told her after I repeated the queries a couple of times, "Listen, I am going to go get in line to pay. That is a lot of fruit. You decide which one you are keeping and come on over to the checkout line."

She came over to the checkout line and I asked her, "So you made a decision?"

She said, "Yes, Ma'am, I kept them all."

I paid for all of the fruit, and we carried the bags to the car and headed back to the house.

The music was playing and I reached to turn it down because a question had been placed in my mind - Peter Moment. I asked her, "May I ask you a question?"

She started laughing out loud. I said smiling, "What is so funny?"

She responded by saying, "You have already asked me a lot of questions?"

I said, "Correct. May I ask you another question?"

She said, "Yes."

I asked, "Do you think the God we serve could make your taste buds so large that you could love all of those fruits I just purchased for the fruit salad?"

She said, "Yes, you know what you say – God can do anything."

I said, "Hear me when I say this to you. I am not trying to take your mother's place in your life. She will always be your mother. As a matter of fact, she did me a favor by having you and your brother with your father. She saved me the trouble of having to get fat, out of shape and pregnant."

"Question: Do you think God made your heart large enough to love more than one person if He made your tiny taste buds love all of that fruit?"

Her response was silence. We arrived back at the house. We did not speak of our conversation again, nor did I allow myself to be alone with her—not sure if it was intentional or coincidental.

After their departure from the weekend's visitation, I shared the conversation with Art, and I told him I do not know where the questions came from and I had no idea what the answers would be. God was the only answer that I had for the questions and the fruit analogy. Never, never had anyone ever shared that act, nor had I read about it being performed to teach a heart its depth.

Two weeks later they arrived as scheduled, and she was the first person to run into the house. I was waiting to be greeted standing in my dutiful attitude – thinking "What is up with her, today?"

She came in, greeted me and was falling over her words talking so fast about this or that. I asked her to slow down. She said, "I thought about the questions you asked me in the car?"

I was clueless as to what she was referring. I had not thought much about our shopping trip after talking with Art.

She said, "The questions you asked me about God making my heart large enough to love more than one person?"

"Yes, I recall," was my response.

She said, "I know the answer. God did make my heart big enough to love more than one person, just like it is okay to like or love all those different fruits."

I hugged her and she hugged me back. It was not happily ever after, but the fruit and the heart had a meeting of the minds. She began to try to accept and receive the love I was offering her. I could only thank God for being God.

"Not an on-time God but a beforehand God" jrn

He already had a plan, and I just had to be obedient.

Yesterday, in our blended family I was called Ms. Jay. Today, I am called Mommy J. Here is the trick—I answer to it. It took a little adjusting for me, but my stepdaughter kept using the title she had chosen for me. (Mary was chosen, Joseph was chosen, now Ms. Jay was chosen).

The Trojan Horse

The cliché "experience is a good teacher" can be the one cliché that could practically be applied to anyone's life in one stage or another. "Why?" – You might ask. Well, if you hear, see or read about something successful or not successful, it may assist in the direction you choose to move toward or move away from.

Have you read or heard the Greek Myth story about the Trojan War story? We would like to show how this story can be compared to the stepparents, biological parents and the other biological parents' wars.

War paraphrased is when at least two groups want power or disagree. These two groups disagree about something that could include prejudice, land, money, sex, words, choices or even the colors you may wear.

A war does not have to be with hundreds or thousands of people. It may be as small as one person. People are in constant conflict with themselves, and I personally believe they also inflict their conflict on others.

The Trojan War, Greek mythology, is a war between the Greeks and the people of Troy. The strife began after the **Trojan** Prince Paris abducted Helen, wife of Menelaus of Sparta. When Menelaus demanded her return, the **Trojans** refused. Menelaus then persuaded his brother Agamemnon to lead an army against Troy. Details of this story are shared in the margin.

TROJAN WAR STORY

Trojan Prince Paris (A Greek) wanted to marry Helen, the beautiful wife of a Greek king, so he took her to Troy, the city. (Trojan Took)

Greek King Menelaus wanted his wife back. He went to Troy and attacked the city. However, the Greeks could not enter Troy because there was a strong wall around the city. (Greek – Get Helen Back)

The Trojans and Greeks fought for many years (10) because of Helen. Finally, the goddess Athena told the **Greeks** to build a big wooden horse to hide in. Many soldiers hid in the horse

Greeks did not know how to get the horse into the city Troy. A Greek soldier called Sinon had an idea. He told the other Greek soldiers to sail away in their boats.

Then he told the Trojans that all the Greeks had left and sailed away. He said the horse was a gift for Athena, the Greek goddess.

The Trojans believed Sinon. They pulled the big wooden horse into the city. Then they celebrated and went to sleep.

During the night, the Greek soldiers came out of the horse and attacked the Trojans. They killed many people and burned the city.

The Greeks took Helen back to her husband. Aeneas was one of a few Trojans who survived. He escaped the city with his father and his son. They went to a hill and watched their city burn. Finally, the Trojan War was over.

Wars are never good, but sometimes they are necessary to stop the power struggle and establish peace and yes, peace of mind counts. Various tools are used when warring, for example **deceit**: People often use deceit to get what they want. They lie to others to trick them.

In this story, Sinon deceived the Trojans. He lied to them about the Greeks leaving. He also lied to them about the wooden horse. All of his lies and deceit set the Trojans up for defeat. Although the Trojans started the war by taking Helen away, the Trojans should not have believed Sinon so readily, knowing he was Greek – the enemy.

Consider one biological parent to be from Troy and the other the Greeks. If Helen can represent the children, and if the biological parents are in a war over the children after divorce, deceit may be a weapon that is used during this war. Now, we all know that in wars, there are spoils of war.

According to the story, Helen (the children) did not start the war, but the war was about her (them). She did not have a decision in being abducted or returned, just as your children did not have a say about your divorce; yet they become the victims, weapons and used as pawns in the power struggle.

Are you having a war with your X because of your children or stepparent? Are you always defending one of the three sectors of your family to the members of your family? Are you seeking a way to be in controlled and not out of control?

If you are finding yourself on the battle fields defending your X's actions to the stepparent, defending your children's actions to your mate or defending your actions to X (biological parent), STOP! You must get on the OFFENSE and PRIORITIZE your ultimate goal. How do you stop? Meditate on the points we have listed below:

- ❖ Understand your rights and the laws as they relate to you and your children.
- ❖ If you do not understand your rights or the law, remember to ASK.
   (A)lways (S)eek (K)nowledge (Ask the right source for the information).
- ❖ Know who you are in war with, why and more importantly, recognize who is fighting on your side.
- ❖ Do not accept any gifts from your enemy.
- ❖ Believe that your opponent will and can be deceitful.
- ❖ Expect the enemy to try to sneak in your camp when you are sleeping
- ❖ Plan and practice your fire drill.

Fire Drill

As children when we were in elementary school and later as adults, we had to learn and participate in fire drills. A fire drill for those of you who are not familiar with the terms is practicing a preparedness plan for when there is a fire.

The following excerpts are taken from the book Introduction to Employee Fire and Life Safety, © 2001 National Fire Protection Association. The two steps that are essential components for fire preparedness are:

(1) An emergency action plan, which details what to do when a fire occurs
(2) A fire prevention plan, which describes what to do to prevent a fire from occurring.

I had embraced the concept of the fire drill's essential components for preparedness to practice before I became a stepparent. After stepping into the role of a stepparent, I put the concept into action even more by being in a constant state of readiness for whatever might come at me.

Since we cannot control the behavior of others and I really had no warning of the hidden arrows coming at me, I had to make sure I had on my armor. I had to have a plan, and I had to plan ahead if anyone decided to act like a clown in my presence or my absence. This was critical; there was an X to contend with, children of divorce, and we were in a new relationship. There was going to be conflict and some unseemly behavior. Now don't get me wrong—clowns play an important role at a circus and parties.

I coined the phrase, "There is a clown in every circus" for when I was presented with unacceptable behavior from my stepchildren, their mother, any friends or family. Just by being prepared, this phrase would bring me humor, diffuse any immediate response or negative action on my part and allow me time to calm waaayyy down.

A classic time to present a fire drill plan that needs to go into action even before the fire alarms start may be the 3rd time your blended family home received an unmerited call from the X at an hour that even an early bird would not appreciate even it was going to get the worm.

If you have already prepared yourself with a practiced acceptable response when the act happens, you are armed and ready. Like "Really! This is your third time calling and the answer remains the same as it was the previous call so make better use of your time and stop wasting mine, please." (Try with a smile but if you must – grit your teeth) ☺

The fire drill plan does not have to come into effect only in your step parenting situation. It is a good practice to use on any occasion when you really know control is required. See examples below:

A. Step parenting:

If you and your lethal weapon (partner) have agreed on a response to a behavior if witnessed and on what your response will be, then your fire drill readiness and prevention act has just been established.

+ Alarm   The signal to inform you a fire may be in progress
+ Fire   The act that is trying to burn at your nerves
+ Water   The way you put it out

B. Life in general:

Suppose you have an associate that is always sharing negative things, just living for the drama. If you already have a plan, use it. Say, "Oh, did you know I am not doing negative right now. Can I schedule you in for when I am available?"

We strongly recommend planning ahead and preempt your responses to fiery behavior. If you don't plan ahead, you may get left behind in the smoke of "Oh, No, they did not? Not again? UUUGH!!!!!"

Why have a fire drill practice in school, home, or work? So you will not have to think what to do in a real situation, and no instruction will be required. However, you may need or be given some directions.

So, Jay, what is the difference between instructions and directions? That is a really good question. According to www.differencebetween.net the summary listed below is a precise answer:

1. Both "directions" and "instructions" are a series of orders or steps to gain a result. In addition, both are words that imply knowledge. Latin Roots and can be presented in an oral and written presentation
2. Directions are considered to be less forceful than instructions. Navigational cues are examples.
3. Instructions are guidelines on how to do something while directions are designed for what to do.

Ways to Show Appreciation for Stepparents

Would you clock into work for a 40-50 hour-a-week job, and later find out that you will not be getting paid? What if you went to work for months? Then months turned into years? And no PAY! No Cheese? No Cash Money?

Jesus was a gift for mankind, but He knew that He, for the least, would be returning home to God, the Father, where there were many mansions. He also knew that He was in the position to prepare a place for those that believed.

No one wants to go to work and not get PAID! The rich ask for a sum of payment. It may not be dollars. It could be a tax break. The middle class wants to get paid, and the poor wants some type of tender whether it be food, money, clothes, or even a place to stay.

That is not a bad thing. It is a good and acceptable way of living. If you go to work, you should get paid. You agree to a tender with terms and if you do your part then you expect the other party to do theirs. According to dictionary.com the word appreciation is defined as: *1.gratitude; thankful recognition: They showed their appreciation by giving him a gold watch. 2. the act of estimating the qualities of things and giving them their proper value. 3. clear perception or recognition, especially of aesthetic quality: a course in art appreciation. 4. an increase or rise in the value of property, goods, etc. 5. critical notice; evaluation; opinion, as of a situation, person, etc. 6. a critique or written evaluation, especially when favorable.*

Wow, even the definition of the words is so broad that it has 6 different senses. I guess *six* is not a lot when it is compared to the word *set*. The word *set* is only a three-letter word but it has 430 senses, requiring a sixty-word-definition spread over 24 pages in the tiny print of the published dictionary or 221 pages in PDF form. In a nutshell, the word *appreciation* itself says that the ways to show appreciation are not limited to our list or beyond your imagination.

Step parenting is just like clocking into work and not getting paid. You have no legal rights in regard to making decisions for the stepchildren at school, hospital, taxes or natural beneficiary, etc., unless you have adopted children which is less likely than more. If you are one of the lucky ones to obtain rights, you have to pay for them even if you earn them. If you willingly are taking care of stepchildren, the courts may demand that you continue or consider you to be a nonrelated outsider and you have absolutely no rights at all.

"You can PAY as a stepparent but you have no SAY!" JamArt

Make a consolidated effort to try to remove the "sting" of step parenting by creating bright lights in the darkness. In other words, go out of your way to show appreciation to the chosen stepparent. Make the stepparent know that he or she is of value and not just of need, love, or convenience. Just like there are thousands of ways to show your love, hate, honor, or dislike, there are thousands of ways to show appreciation to the stepparent. Guess what? Many of the ways that I was shown appreciation did not cost anything but time. These are but a few ways that Art showed his appreciation for me being his children's stepmother. Art wrote the book on showing his appreciation to my dedication and love for him and his children. I never did develop an appreciation for his X.

As quiet as it has been kept - shhhhhh: I REALLY HAVE A PROBLEM WITH HER NOT HAVING HIS BEST INTEREST AT HEART WHEN HE WAS ALWAYS GOING BEYOND EXPECTATIONS FOR THEIR CHILDREN AND SOMETIMES HER. I was convinced she was living with regret losing him and all he brought to the table for her and their children.

I did not win all of the battles presented to me as a stepparent, but I was determined to win the war. I did not want to witness another really good man (and readers when I tell a really **good Man** with not one, not even a half of one malicious (bad) bone in his body or mind) to be taken for granted because he wanted simply to be a good father to his children, successfully survive divorce and secure a loving relationship with a woman (me) who could love him and his children to levels beyond his greatest expectation.

- He listened with understanding of my position

- He understood without judgment

- He found ways to squeeze in gestures of appreciation during the kids' visitation. For example:

  o Running a hot bath with candles and music accent
  o Breakfast, lunch and sometimes dinner would be served in the bed

- o Flowers, fresh sometimes, and when the money was not as plentiful, he would bring in flowers from the yard
  - o Candy – sometimes the top shelf candy and sometimes a snicker bar with almonds – my favorite

- I love music—jazz, gospel and RB… He would be willing to go to a free concert in the park, when he really did not like being outside on the grass.

  - o Buy CD (or download a .99 cents song)
  - o Find a live jazz show on TV, DVD or XM and set up as we going to a show
  - o Back Rub
  - o Massage
  - o Foot Rub
  - o An unexpected hug in front of the children

Coffee … OMG! If you love coffee like I do then you would understand. He could come back after a survival weekend with the children with DD's coffee, and the world would look all the better to me. The list goes on….

  - o Road Trip … to family or friends' home just overnight sometimes
  - o Go to the park
  - o Write a note on a post-it and set it out to be seen
  - o Say the words … "Thank you!"
  - o Try putting in a helping hand in preparation and departure
  - o Do some of the chores that were left behind
  - o Sometimes just provide his presence in the same room
  - o Play a game (he is not a game player)
  - o A Teddy Bear might show itself in the door saying Hi
  - o Try to tell a Joke (this was not his strong point)
  - o Make a card
  - o Take a ride away from the house if it was just to the grocery store to change to scenery.
  - o Buy a perfect card and add his own words to bring the card closer to his words in feeling. (Some men aren't big talkers but that does not mean you can't say a lot with a few words.)
  - o Do something out of ordinary like putting something on his head and when you look up … and all you can do is smile

- He would have pre-conversations with the children prior to arrival, and eventually they understood that we were not changing our plan about our love; if they wanted to be a part of it, they would respect and accept it. They did not have to like it, but if he had to choose, they may lose more of his time.
- We would like to share some of the cards purchased for me from Art in the picture below. *He could really melt my attitude with those cards.

In addition, he informed the children of the changes he had made in his life just so their living conditions, lifestyles and wellbeing could remain as close to little change as possible. Sharing this type of information with the children gave them a foundation and frame of reference to be able to recognize false accusations and misinformation from the X factor and others.

I did not take him or his acts of appreciation for granted. I welcomed them, and I am blessed for it.

Our greatest treasure was and is EACH OTHER.

We recognized after all the smoke had cleared from the fires associated with step parenting and divorced daddy parenting that we, (Art and I), were not disagreeing over "us." Our conflicts were over the children, the X factor and the unexpected behavior.

FACT 19:   *"Distractions keep you away from your Attractions" jrn*

(My Card Tree of Appreciation- light shining through the dark shades)

Words & Closing Thoughts

Words have an unbelievable important power in our lives. The beginnings of the majority of all relationships, good, bad, ugly or indifferent, begin with words. In the book of John, the very first sentence of the first chapter supports this line of thinking:

1 In the beginning was the Word, and the Word was with God, and the Word was God.

Did you notice that the *word* "word" itself was used in this same sentence three times? If you recall, God spoke words for the creation, Genesis 1:

Genesis 1 (KJV): 3 And God said, Let there be light: and there was light. … 6 And God said, Let there be a firmament in the midst of the waters, and let it divide the waters from the waters.

Proverbs 18:21 (KJV): 21 Death and life are in the power of the tongue: and they that love it shall eat the fruit thereof.

John 1 (KJV): 1 In the beginning was the Word, and the Word was with God, and the Word was God. 2 The same was in the beginning with God.

According to Merriam-Webster dictionary the full definition of "WORD":

1a : something that is said b plural (1) : talk, discourse <putting one's feelings into words> (2) : the text of a vocal musical composition c : a brief remark or conversation 3a (1) : a speech sound or series of speech sounds that symbolize and communicate a meaning usually without being divisible into smaller units capable of independent use (2) : the entire set of linguistic forms produced by combining a single base with various inflectional elements without change in the part of speech elements b (1) : a written or printed character or combination of characters representing a spoken word (2) : any segment of written or printed discourse ordinarily appearing between spaces or between a space and a punctuation mark 3: order, command

Words that are positive, influential, good feeling, encouraging speak life. The opposite words speak death and with that being said, we would like to add one additional positive note:

While you are blending the different notes that will accompany your journey of a blended family, loving your chosen mate and simply just making the best of your decisions, words will have a resounding sound in the minds of your listeners and even in your own thoughts. So choose your words wisely.

FACT 20:   The words that you choose to use will make a big difference in how you are heard, understood, misunderstood, appreciated, respected, disrespected, loved, disliked, desired, -this list can be as long as infinity. Words have an unbelievably important power in our lives.

We have selected a group of positive words from a website (below), our vocabulary and the dictionary to assist in guiding the chosen words you may select when addressing the issues of step parenting or showing your appreciation for the stepparent. There are at least 1,100 positive words that you can include in your vocabulary; however, we only listed a few of them. The first letters of each word would represent each letter in the title of this book – Lethal Weapon.

Lethal Weapon

Positive words starting with letter L:

like, laugh – laughing, learn – learning, life, live – living, luxury, longevity, loyalty – loyal, love – lovable – loving, liberty, logic, leader – leadership, luck – lucky, light, loving-kindness, lively, life of the party, lovely, loving acceptance, loving feelings

Positive words starting with letter E:

empathy – empathize – emphatic, easy – easily, educate – education – educated, efficient, enable – enabled, energetic – energize – energy, engage – engaging – engaged, enjoy – enjoyment, enough, eager – eagerness, effectiveness, efficiency, elation, elegance, encourage – encouragement – encouraged

Positive words starting with letter T:

true, trust – trusting , tact, teach – teachable, team, thankful – thank – thank-you – thankfulness, therapy, time, teamwork, timeliness, tolerance, tradition, tranquil – tranquility, trust, truth – truthfulness, tender, thrilled, touch – touched, tickled, to matter, to know, to be known, to be seen, transformative – transformation – transform, triumph, teamwork, thrive – thriving, tenacity

Positive words starting with letter H:

hope – hopefulness, happiness – happy – happily, harmonious – harmonize – harmony, health – healthy, heart, hello, help – helpful – helping, hot – honest – honesty, human, humor, helpfulness, hero – heroism, holy – holiness, honesty, honor, hospitality, humble, heaven – heavenly, halo

Positive words starting with letter A:

able, accept – acceptance – acceptable – accepted – accepting, action, activate, active, add, addition, admirable, adorable, advantage, affirm, ageless, agree, agreeable, aid, aim, abundance, accountability, accomplishment – accomplish, accuracy, achievement – achieve, acknowledgement, adaptability, adventure – adventurous, agility

Positive words starting with letter L:

like, laugh – laughing, learn – learning, life, live – living, luxury, longevity, loyalty – loyal, love – lovable – loving, liberty, logic, leader – leadership, luck – lucky, light, loving-kindness, lively, life of the party, lovely, loving acceptance, loving feelings,

Positive words starting with letter W:

worth – worthy – worthiness, wealth, warm – warmth, welcome, will- willing – willingness , wisdom, wise, won, wonderful, well-being, wholeheartedness, wow, wonder, water, well, wellness, welfare, whole, wonder-working, win – winnable – winning

Positive words starting with letter E:

empathy – empathize – emphatic, easy – easily, educate – education – educated, efficient, enable – enabled, energetic – energize – energy, engage – engaging – engaged, enjoy – enjoyment, enough, eager – eagerness, effectiveness, efficiency, elation, elegance, encourage – encouragement – encouraged, endurance, equality, excellence – excellent, excite – excitement – excited, experience, expertise, exploration, expressiveness expressing, enlightenment, eternal, exaltation, emulate

Positive words starting with letter A:

able, accept – acceptance – acceptable – accepted – accepting, action, activate, active, add, addition, admirable, adorable, advantage, affirm, ageless, agree, agreeable, aid, aim, abundance, accountability, accomplishment – accomplish, accuracy, achievement – achieve, acknowledgement, adaptability, adventure – adventurous, agility, alertness, ambition, anticipation, appreciate – appreciation – appreciative – appreciativeness, assertiveness – assertive, attentiveness, audacity

Positive words starting with letter P:

perfect – perfection, positive energy, positive thoughts, positive events, positive circumstances, positive beliefs, peace – pacify, paradise – paradisiac, passion – passionate, please, pure, peace, perceptiveness, perseverance, persistence, personal growth, pleasure, positive attitude, positive words, power – powerful, practicality, precision, preparedness

Positive words starting with letter O:

optimist – optimistic, outstanding, ok, on, onwards, open – openly – opening, open-minded, opportunity, original, openness, opportunity, optimism, order, organization, originality, outcome, orientation, obedient, open hearted, omg, overcome, om mani padme hum, outgoing, oneness, outer nationalist

Positive words starting with letter N:

noble, nurturing – nurture, non-resistance – non-resistant, new, nice, nirvana, noble, neat, nature-made, nourish – nourished – nourishing – nourishment, namaste, neoteny

http://positivewordsresearch.com/list-of-positive-words

After reading these positive words "L-e-t-h-a-l W-e-a-p-o-n", do you feel good? If so, read them often. If not, try reading the words again and focus on their meanings and impact.

[Art's 20-20 Hindsight: Communication Styles]

Jay and I realized that we were not mind readers of each other's thoughts, and we also recognized that we have had some similar and some very different life experiences and communicate differently based on these experiences. I had to learn Jay's style of communication. She is a woman of many words – expressive, thoughtful, encouraging, considerate and reasonably literal. So, she had to learn my style of communication because I, on the other hand, a man of few words – brief and to the point. Both of us learned that words do and did play a major role in our success in blending our family. I would like to suggest that you choose and use your words wisely whether they are many or few.

We wish you the best of success while blending your family. We shall bring this book to a close but we remain open to any of our readers', hearers', doers' and haters' contacting us via our website, email: takingthestepoutlw@gmail.com, social media, and our publisher.

[20-20: End]

THANK YOU! And we wish you the best.

Legal Issues of Stepparents

Q & A'S

Did you know that you do not have any legal rights to your stepchildren?

Did you know, stepparent, that you can obtain a medical release form to authorize you to be able to authorize medical treatment for a minor child?

Did you know, stepparents, that if you are cohabiting adults and not married by law, you can use a lease agreement to protect you from having to pay child support for your stepchildren?

Did you know if you are granted the permission to add your stepchildren to your taxes because you cared financially for them that you should get a statement from the children's parents and have it notarized to show proof if needed by IRS.

Did you know you can adopt your stepchildren? You will have to obtain permission from both biological parents

Did you know you have a right to get respect from your stepchildren?

- The Bible tells you so
- You already know if you demand it at home, it might show up outside of the home

Legal Issues

Stepfamily marriages are a little different in the eyes of the law. Most couples go into a marriage that has stepchildren hoping to make up for or deal with the pain and suffering endured from their previous family. A few perils need to be considered by everyone involved in the stepfamily and custodial parent. This article will help you identify some of the perils and offer suggestions to minimize them.

Legal Status of Stepparents and Stepchildren

Law does not acknowledge a stepparent. This makes it difficult for stepparents who want to take care of the children. Sometimes when a stepparent goes beyond his stepparent role, it usually creates a problem. This includes anything that the biological parent would tolerate or allow. To avoid any problems in the future, it is a good idea to outline the amount of discipline and love that should be shown between the stepparent and children involved.

Most stepparents will apply the same type of parenting skills that they are already familiar with and this is not wrong but if it is different from the biological parents then this may lead to a battle down the road.

This may be very difficult for the stepparent who wants to be a part of the child's life and not be so restricted. When the stepparent acts instead of the biological parent, they may be denied rights that a biological parent has. For example – medical treatment.

If the stepparent does not have a medical document release form stating that they are allowed to authorize treatment for the minor children, then they will be denied. This form can be obtained by an attorney who will prepare the form and then have both the custodial parent and the non-custodial parent, when able to sign. When authorization is needed for schools or school related functions and other times when a stepparent wants or needs authorization, a similar paper can be used. It is important that a stepparent's role in a child's life is clearly written for his or her protection.

A Stepparent's Will and the Stepchild's Inheritance Rights

At some time in a couple's life, it will be necessary to discuss a will. According to the law, a stepchild has no right to a stepparent's inheritance. If the stepparent dies and does not have a will, then the stepchild will not be able to receive any portion of the estate in question. If you want to make sure that the stepchild receives a portion of the estate, then a will must clearly state what the stepchild should receive.

When a biological parent feels that his or her child is being treated unfairly as a stepchild in the will when there are biological children involved, then this situation must be handled in a rational manner. Although this is a very emotional time for everyone, it is something that should be worked out as a family.

Child Support Responsibilities of the Biological Parent

Another issue that is a concern of a stepparent is child support issues. A stepparent may feel as though she or he is paying for expenses that are the responsibility of the biological parent. In order to solve the problem, a stepparent would need to take the parent of the child back to court to see if child support payments need to be readjusted.

The situations listed above are unique in stepfamilies. This can be very stressful to a marriage and can lead to divorce. When a divorce is final, a stepparent has no role in the child's life anymore, and there cannot be any child support ordered. The same goes for child custody and visitations.

If you are a stepparent, protect yourself for the future. Stepfamilies can provide a happy and loving home to children who can learn from a successful marriage and family lifestyle that you provide.

- The content of this page is provided for informational purposes only. If you need advice regarding a family law issue, talk to a family lawyer near you.

State Laws Regarding Stepparent Rights and Obligations, by: Susan L. Pollet, Esq.

According to the statistics, approximately 50% of U.S. marriages end in divorce, 60% of second marriages end in divorce and about 43% of marriages are remarriages for at least one party. While the statistics vary, estimates are that as many as one in three American children now can expect to spend some of their childhood years living with a stepparent. A stepparent has been defined as a person married to the legal (natural or adoptive) parent of a child. There are stepparents who legally adopt their stepchildren and they are treated as biological parents under the law. A more expansive definition of a stepparent includes live-in girlfriends and boyfriends.

For at least the last decade, legal commentators have noted that while stepparents often play an important role in their stepchildren's lives, overall there is a lack of legal recognition of the stepparent/stepchild relationship. It has been argued that residential stepparents generally have fewer rights than legal guardians or foster parents.

With regard to custody and visitation rights, courts generally have less difficulty awarding a stepparent visitation rather than custody. Only about one-third of states provide for visitation by stepparents in their legislation. All of the statutes contain a requirement, either expressly or implicitly, that visitation must be in the best interests of the child and some state laws impose additional conditions.

With regard to child support, at common law, the relationship of stepparent and stepchild did not, of itself, confer any rights or impose any duties. A stepparent is obligated to support a stepchild during the marriage where there is a statute imposing such a duty or the stepparent undertakes to act in loco parentis to the child. There are states with specific statutes dealing with the issue and in certain states, if a stepparent voluntarily received a stepchild into his or her family and treated the stepchild as a member thereof, he or she could be placed in loco parentis and assume an obligation to maintain and support the child.

With regard to inheritance rights, a commentator noted that the large majority of people die intestate and thus state law rather than a will, determines who inherits a decedent's estate. Consequently, unadopted stepchildren often do not inherit from their stepparents because most intestacy schemes limit distribution of a decedent's estate to individuals who were either related to a decedent by blood or were legally adopted by a decedent. Stepparents always have the option to write wills in which they can specifically provide their unadopted stepchildren with inheritance rights no matter which type of relationship the stepfamilies form.

See more at: http://www.babymed.com/law-legal/state-laws-regarding-stepparent-rights-and-obligations

Rights of Stepparents in Custody and Visitation

The rights of a stepparent to request custody or visitation of children who are not his or her natural children can be challenging. On some levels, the law treats a stepparent similarly to a natural parent in examining the parent's relationship to the children and his or her significance in the children's life, rather than focusing solely on the source of DNA. Considerations do not end there, however. Before a stepparent can petition for visitation rights or custody in some circumstances, the hurdle of standing must be mounted.

What is "Standing"?

Standing refers to the rights of a party to be heard by courts on a particular issue. The determination of standing involves consideration of several factors:

- Degree of the stepparent's participation at a significant level in the children's life

- Length of time the stepparent participated as an actual parent for the children in place of the children's natural parent

- Existence of any relationship and emotional ties between stepparent and children

- Amount of financial support and assistance provided by the stepparent

- Degree of detriment to the children if the stepparent is denied visitation

In most cases, stepparents are deemed not to have access to the divorce proceeding in court. Instead, courts hold that divorce laws, which establish their jurisdiction to adjudicate custody matters within the divorce, do not grant further jurisdiction to hear cases between parents and stepparents over custody. Occasionally, a court will decide such disputes but with rarity.

Visitation Heard More Readily Than Custody

Despite these challenges, some courts have expressed a willingness to decide visitation matters more readily than custody disputes. One reason is due to the underlying liberal visitation statutes.

Recently, advocates have leaned strongly on their state legislators and legal systems to enact laws granting visitation rights to grandparents, especially in instances of divorce or death of one parent. Grandparent visitation statutes have been enacted in response. Stepparents seek the same rights and protections within the legal system to safeguard their relationships with their children although a birth relationship or bloodline does not exist.

Today, nearly half the states (23) have enacted laws to authorize stepparent visitation. Ten more states expressly granted stepparents rights to seek visitation. Thirteen additional states grant interested third parties rights to request visitation and deem stepparents as fitting within the "interested third party" definition. In the absence of state statutes on point, some courts have held that stepparents may still petition for visitation. Four states, Alabama, Florida, Iowa, and South Dakota, foreclose this right entirely to stepparents.

Legal Standard Applicable to Stepparent's Visitation Request

Regardless of the state, most courts use the "best interests of the children" test to determine whether to award a stepparent requested visitation. Courts review whether continuing the children's relationship with a stepparent enhances the children's life and improves his or her welfare. If the answer is "yes", visitation is awarded. If there are questions about the fitness of the stepparent, visitation rights may be curtailed or denied.

Rights, Responsibilities and Liabilities of a Stepparent
by Peter M. Bryniczka

With the prevalence of divorce and the frequency of remarriage, blended families with stepparents and stepchildren are a common feature of modern domestic society. Ideally, stepparents develop closely bonded relationships with their stepchildren and, vice versa, providing an additional support system for the children of divorce. These children experience extreme dislocations, both physical and emotional, even when the divorce is as low conflict and amicable as can be.

The beneficial influence of mom and/or dad remarrying to a partner who bonds with and cares for their stepchildren cannot be underestimated. Neither can the positive effect of the children's being a key part of two new integral and stable families (i.e., mom and stepdad and dad and stepmom). Again, ideally, the children now have four parents (two biological and two stepparents) to love, nurture, help, support, advise and set an example for them. Although this admittedly only scratches the surface of the stepparent/stepchildren dynamic, it might be surprising to realize that the law does not afford any special status to stepparent's vis-à-vis their stepchildren.

When biological parents divorce or part ways (if never married), the law in every state sets forth detailed provisions about each parent's rights and duties. These laws provide a framework for how the courts shall intervene when parents cannot agree on issues related to their children. The courts are even empowered to make decisions as to what is in the children's best interests when and if the parents cannot agree. Simply put, the law affords biological parents who divorce or part ways with a well scripted guide full of procedures, rules, and parameters for resolving children-related disputes. However, this is not at all the case for a stepparent.

Stepparents have no rights

Biological parents may divorce each other but they do not divorce their children. They don't stop seeing, caring for, nurturing, loving and raising their children. Nor does divorce eliminate a parental obligation to care for and support one's children. But what happens when the marriage between a biological parent and stepparent ends?

What happens to the relationship forged between stepparent and children, perhaps over many years? Is the stepparent expected simply to walk away, even if that is exactly what the biological parent wants? What about the effects on the children of abruptly ending what was (hopefully) a strong and positive bonded relationship with this stepparent?

Unlike a divorce between biological parents in which the children will continue to have both parents firmly in his or her life, the divorce of a biological parent from a stepparent is more comparable to the death of a loved one because the stepparent is essentially, from the standpoint of the children, here one day and gone the next. A degree in psychology is not a prerequisite to appreciating the extreme negative effects this can and often does have on a child.

In an ideal world, a biological parent who is divorcing the stepparent would be well aware of the bonds forged between his or her children and the stepparent and would recognize that supporting the children's continued contact and relationship with the (now former) stepparent would be beneficial to the children. (This, of course, assumes that the children and stepparent did, in fact, enjoy the ideal stepparent-children relationship.) However, the world is unfortunately not ideal. Just as biological parents embroiled in a divorce (or the aftermath of a divorce) often forget, minimize, and/or deny the importance an estranged or former spouse has had in the lives of their children, so too does the biological parent with respect to the role the stepparent has played.

A very important distinction, however, is that biological parents have a well-scripted legal landscape by which to assert and preserve their rights, even absent acknowledgment by the other parent. What does the stepparent have? Nothing.

Another permutation of this issue is when a biological parent dies during an intact marriage to a stepparent. Where does that leave the stepparent with respect to the stepchildren? What if the children's surviving biological parent is unwilling to allow the children any further contact with the stepparent? Or worse yet, what happens if both biological parents die? What then? These are potentially scary and unsettling questions that no stepparent hopes ever to face. But each year, many stepparents face exactly these questions and there are often no satisfactory answers.

The Impact of Troxel

Each state makes its own laws with respect to divorce and the financial and children-related aspects of divorce. Therefore, what follows is a discussion of the law generally as it exists among the states. While many legal tenets of family law are similar from state to state (especially in the financial area), the law can and does differ significantly from one state to the next. Talk with your lawyer about the law in your state.

Generally, across all states, stepparents are afforded no special legal status. Instead, the law treats a stepparent seeking custody or visitation of stepchildren as any other unrelated third-party. Grandparents who seek custody or visitation of their grandchildren, against the wishes of the children's parents, find themselves in a similar predicament. Any discussion of third-party visitation and/or custodial rights begins with the June 5, 2000, U.S. Supreme Court decision of Troxel v. Granville, 530 U.S. 57(2000).

In the Troxel case, a biological parent objected to a stepparent's request for more expansive visitation. After a trial and appeal, the case went to the U.S. Supreme Court.

The Supreme Court found that the Washington State nonparental visitation statute (on which the Troxel petition was based) was "breathtakingly broad" to the point of unconstitutionally infringing upon the protection afforded by the Fourteen Amendment against governmental interference with fundamental rights—specifically, the interest of parents in the care, custody, and control of their children, including the presumption that fit parents act in the best interests of their children. The Court indicated that such a right of parents is "perhaps the oldest of the fundamental liberty interests recognized by [the U.S. Supreme Court]."

Therefore, in every state, whenever the rights of third-parties (including stepparents) are involved (whether relying on state statute or case law), the law must bow to, and evolve in light of, the U.S. Supreme Court's decision in Troxel v. Granville.

Special weight must be afforded the decisions made by fit parents as to whether their children will visit and/or have a relationship with third parties. Thus, nonparental third parties have a significant uphill battle to wage in seeking access to children, not their own, against the wishes of the children's parents. It is in this unenviable position that nonparental third parties have a significant uphill battle in seeking access to children, not their own, against the wishes of the children's parents stepparents seeking to gain visitation with former stepchildren find themselves. Again, knowing how the law in your state has evolved since the Troxel decision is paramount.

A very interesting and important question in terms of the evolution of state law as to third-party access was specifically not reached by the U.S. Supreme Court in Troxel: Does the Due Process Clause of the U.S. Constitution require a showing of harm, or potential harm, to the children as a condition for granting third-party visitation?

State law often evolves to fill in this blank. Knowing the particulars for your state is a key part of the inquiry. For example, in Connecticut, the case law and statutory law evolved after Troxel to require that a third party seeking visitation with children must prove that (a) a "parent like" relationship exists between the person and the children; and (b) that denial of visitation would result in real and significant harm to the children.

Financial liability

Now, turning to a very different aspect of being a stepparent is whether a stepparent is financially liable for the support of stepchildren. For purposes of asserting custody and visitation rights toward stepchildren, stepparents are, likewise, not responsible under the law for the direct support of their stepchildren.

Unlike a biological parent who has a legal duty to support his or her children, there is no collateral legal obligation of a stepparent to support unrelated stepchildren.

However, there is the potential, again depending on the particulars of state law, for a stepparent to potentially be indirectly involved in the support of stepchildren.

For example, imagine a situation in which Dad is divorced from Mom. They have children. Child support orders are put in place at the time of the divorce, based on Mom's and Dad's financial circumstances at that time.

A few years after the divorce, Dad remarries Stepmom and they commence living together and sharing expenses. Both Dad and Stepmom are employed. Mom files a motion asking the court to increase Dad's children support paid to her because his living expenses have now been significantly reduced due to Stepmom's financial contributions to the household and, thus, Dad has more income available for children support than when he was single and living on his own.

The law of your state will provide whether and to what degree Mom has a case in the above example. Also note that the question of whether and how a stepparent's financial contributions to the household affect a spouse's financial exposure to an ex-spouse will likely be different for alimony and for children support issues.

This article does not attempt to cover the alimony angle. Presumably, the law will regard Stepmom as a separate financial entity with no obligation financially toward her stepchildren and, as such, Stepmom's income cannot directly factor into Dad's children support.

However, there may be some angle under the law, and in some circumstances, in which Mom has a case and will have a right to conduct financial discovery of Dad's assets, expenses, and income and, perhaps, also Stepmom's, at least to some degree. Discovery laws are generally broader than the evidence that might ultimately be admissible at trial.

Mom will likely have the right to explore whether and how Dad's financial union with Stepmom, including some information acquired directly from Stepmom, has effected Dad's finances.

The allowable disclosure from Stepmom will be in proportion to the degree that the children support laws of the particular state consider resources contributed by the stepparent.

For example, in my state, Connecticut, our children support laws would exclude Stepmom's income in calculating Dad's income for children support purposes, but would allow a court to consider to some degree any regularly recurring contributions or gifts from a spouse or domestic partner, provided it is established that the parent has reduced his or her income or experienced an extraordinary reduction in living expenses as a direct result of such contributions or gifts.

Knowing the law in your jurisdiction is crucial to assessing how a stepparent and his or her spouse should handle their financial relationship if potential exposure to a (litigious) ex-spouse may be of concern. Again, most, if not all, states presumably shield a stepparent, at least to some degree. Thus, ask your lawyer how your state approaches the question.

Estate planning

In a typical second marriage, it is very likely that one or both parties will have children from a prior relationship. The new couple also may have children together. Whether or not stepparents have biological children of their own (from a prior or the current relationship), estate planning will likely involve a decision as to whether they want stepchildren to inherit something directly upon their deaths or indirectly at some point thereafter. Which estate planning path is selected will almost certainly depend on whether the stepparent wishes to provide for biological children from the current or a prior relationship, the length of the second marriage, whether children were born of this second marriage, the wealth of each spouse, how long the stepparent has participated in parenting the stepchildren, and the nature and quality of those relationships.

The manner in which title to assets is held is an important first consideration and each spouse should hold specific and sufficient assets in his or her own name in order for any options in the estate planning documents to effectively distribute assets among each spouse's intended group of beneficiaries, including a spouse, children, and/or stepchildren. Conversely, assets held jointly with a spouse with rights of survivorship would pass directly to the joint owner and be outside the operation and control of estate planning documents. In similar fashion, retirement accounts, assets in irrevocable trusts, and life insurance proceeds pass directly to the named beneficiaries and also are outside the control of estate planning documents.

Because leaving all assets to a surviving spouse in a second marriage may not be desired, each spouse should consider what portion of assets should be left to the spouse and what portion should be left to biological children from the current and/or prior relationship, and, perhaps even to stepchildren. Both federal and most state estate tax laws allow a 100% marital deduction or exemption from federal estate tax for assets left to a surviving spouse who is a U.S. citizen via a will, beneficiary designations (e.g. Retirement accounts), and/or by joint ownership with rights of survivorship.

This 100% marital deduction also applies to assets left to the surviving spouse via a qualified terminable interest trust (QTIP trust). To qualify for the 100% marital deduction, such trusts must comply with specific requirements, including that all income of the trust be distributed to the surviving spouse during his or her lifetime. After the death of the surviving spouse and payment of any deferred taxes, the trust can direct assets to the children or even stepchildren of the first spouse to die (i.e., the person who created the trust and whose assets originally went into the trust), in whatever proportion, at whatever times, and subject to whatever further instructions and/or restrictions are specified in the QTIP trust document.

In a second marriage, another common estate-planning option is a federal unified credit for estate and gift taxes used to fund a "credit shelter trust or by-pass trust". Such trusts can benefit one or more of a group of beneficiaries (including a spouse, children, and/or stepchildren) in whatever fashion and per whatever restrictions are written into the trust document. Often such trusts provide for income and occasionally some principal to be paid to the surviving spouse during his or her lifetime and also to the decedent's children (and perhaps even stepchildren) based on need and other instructions in the trust. Upon the surviving spouse's death, the balance of the credit shelter trust would be distributed estate tax-free to the children of the first spouse to die and/or to their stepchildren if desired. Spouses should consult estate-planning attorneys about specific estate-planning options. Each spouse must decide how much and from what sources monies should go directly to the surviving spouse (and/or children and/or stepchildren) and what amounts will be placed into trust (such as the QTIP or credit shelter options). Trusts provide an excellent mechanism by which the maker can direct and control what portions of assets will eventually pass to children and/or stepchildren, while still making provision for a surviving spouse. For the stepparent, all desired estate-planning outcomes can be achieved, provided a careful eye and attention is turned to proper estate-planning, as described above. While intestacy laws make provision for biological descendants and surviving spouses, stepchildren would not factor in at all. Thus, ensuring that stepchildren get something on the death of the stepparent requires some level of estate planning.

A Seamless transition

As a last consideration in the estate-planning vein, for a spouse, parent, or stepparent, the least desirable outcome is for your death and the administration of your estate to create a rift, disputes, or bad-blood between your spouse, your children (from the current and/or a former relationship), and your stepchildren. Careful estate planning for both spouses not only can ensure that assets pass as desired, but also that you are not sowing the seeds of a family dispute. It is also advisable to discuss estate planning with your spouse, your children, and stepchildren (when age appropriate, of course) so that questions and concerns can be identified, addressed, and resolved early in the process. Such discussions also ensure that there are no future surprises for anyone involved.

Peter M. Bryniczka practices law with Schoonmaker, George & Blomberg P.C., in Greenwich, CT.
http://www.sgbfamilylaw.com/pdf/1sum13_bryniczka.pdf

DO I HAVE AN OBLIGATION TO SUPPORT MY STEPCHILDREN?

Dr. Margorie Engel, Ph.D., ©2000*

Confusion about stepparent financial responsibility for stepchildren permeates American society. From our political institutions to our legal codes to the actions and attitudes of individual family members, questions abound with regard to the appropriate and necessary role stepparents should play in the fiscal support of stepchildren.

With respect to financial responsibility for children, no uniform treatment of the stepparent-child relationship exists among the states.

Marriage to a child's parent would seem to create a legal relationship but, to date, this "step" relationship does not typically create rights and obligations between the parties.

Common Law and Stepchild Support

According to common law, stepparents do not have a direct financial responsibility for the health, education, or welfare of their stepchildren. However, if the remarriage ends in divorce, the court notes two possible exceptions for direct financial responsibility to stepchildren by the stepparent in the custodial household: (1) in loco parentis and (2) the "estoppel doctrine".

Typically, in loco parentis is a voluntarily assumed obligation. It is a Latin phrase which means "in lieu of a parent". Teachers, camp counselors, stepparents, and others who take responsibility for children have a duty to act in loco parentis. This means they have the same power and authority over the children as do the parents, at least during the time that the children are under their control.

Millions of stepparents voluntarily provide financial resources for their stepchildren. According to common law, they have a right to be reimbursed by the children's biological father. (I don't know of a case where this has been ordered by the court.) Realistically, time and money bestowed on a stepchild is a gift — of love, or necessity. And if the parent and stepparent later divorce, the stepparent is seldom legally required to provide child support except under specific circumstances.

The Estoppel Doctrine prevents a stepparent from taking a different position or going back on a promise if the child would be financially harmed by the change. It is based on fairness when three conditions exist. The first condition is Representation, as indicated when the stepparent assumes the role of the child's parent — including providing financial support. The second condition is Detriment, describing the stepparent who interferes with the child's relationship with the biological parent and destroys the possibility of obtaining financial support from that parent. The third condition is Reliance, whereby the child relies upon the love and financial support of the stepparent. If these three conditions exist and a divorce occurs, the court may rule that the stepparent is responsible for child support.

By all means, do give love and financial support to your stepchildren. Just don't create a problem for yourself by aggressively interfering with the child's relationship with the biological parent and developing a pattern of paying for a child's necessary expenses when the biological parent is willing and able to do it.

Statutory Law and Financial Support of Stepchildren: State Law of General Applicability

In this usage, state law of "general applicability" refers to a stepparent's obligation to support stepchildren that is equated with the biological parent's obligation to support biological children — support obligations of stepparent and biological parent are coextensive. Some states do include the residential stepparent as a source of support in specified situations; some may even impose criminal penalties upon stepparents who do not fulfill the statutory duty of supporting their stepchildren. Where states have a statute providing that a stepparent has a financial responsibility to support a stepchild, it appears to be based upon the in loco parentis doctrine. Nevertheless, most stepchildren cannot legally claim support from their residential stepparents as few states have enacted statutes to enforce child support obligations on stepparents. (Twenty states do have a statute imposing a financial responsibility on the stepparent while the stepchild is living in the household: DE, HA, IA, KY, ME, MO, NJ, NY, NC, ND, OK, OR, SD, UT, VT, WA.)

Yours, Mine, and Ours: Support of Biological Children and Stepchildren

A stepparent might be in the position of supporting both biological children and stepchildren. This seems most likely to happen if the stepchildren do not receive adequate support payments from the non-custodial parent. Different views about stepchild support exist. Some scholars believe it is only common sense for parents to give priority to the children with whom they live, regardless of whether they are biological children or stepchildren. Court rulings are inconsistent. Some states claim that biological parents cannot reduce child support obligations because of remarriage expenses while others have determined that modification is appropriate.

IRS Exemption

The IRS exemption usually goes to the parent who has physical custody for the greater part of the year — no matter how little either of you actually contribute toward the child's financial support. The IRS recognizes an exception when the custodial parent waives this right. You use IRS Form 8332 to notify the IRS of this waiver. A new form must be completed each year that you want to use the waiver. It must be signed by both parents and filed by the non-custodial parent claiming the exemption.

If you have court ordered joint physical custody, the separation agreement will probably specify which parent is to claim the exemption. Even so, you and your X may agree to one or more "waiver" years without going back to court for a change in your agreement. The operative word is agree. If the court order is silent on the topic of exemption, it automatically goes to the custodial parent. Or, the agreement may specify who will take the exemption. In either case, you and your ex have an opportunity to agree to "exception" years. If there is a tax savings to you as the non-custodial parent, negotiate sharing the savings with your ex-spouse.

Medical Expenses

A child is treated as the dependent of both biological parents, regardless of remarriage status, for purposes of their individual contributions toward medical expenses and reimbursements. Provisions of insurance coverage for children in other households or for residential stepchildren is a gray area. Insurance policies may cover residential stepchildren if they are the income tax dependents of the remarried couple. Read the fine print about limitations, especially if the children are cared for in a joint physical custody arrangement.

Stepfamilies in the Real World

Stepparents are already an important emotional and financial resource for children. Census Bureau projections indicate that more than one-half of today's young people in the United States will become stepsons or stepdaughters in the near future. With so many citizens involved, it seems likely that our states and federal government will need to develop new and specific policies related to stepfamilies. Until a basic social issue has been resolved — nature versus nurture with regard to the care of and responsibility for children — little hope exists of consistent and easily understood family laws and policies or financial security for children.

The courts have had difficulty accepting the possibility that it might be in the child's best interest to have more than two legal parents. However, during a period of high divorce rates, unwed parenthood, couples living together without benefit of a legal document, and recognition that almost half of all marriages are remarriages, it appears that we all are helping to rear each other's children.

As stepparents are already assuming or being given financial responsibility for stepchildren, we must address the issue of specified stepparent custodial rights. Using the doctrine of in loco parentis, this approach recognizes that the natural parent is typically alive and sometimes active as a parent — so a child could officially benefit from two moms and/or two dads who are involved in day-to-day parenting. In this respect, children can, and often do, have more than one mother or father. Whether by law or happenstance, stepparents already have some financial responsibility for stepchildren — what they don't seem to have, however, are rights.

* This article first appeared in Bride Again magazine, summer 2000. Permission granted for use here by Bride Again magazine.

Fact Sheet

List of all of the FACTS denoted in the book:

FACT 1:   Surviving step parenting successfully will be a PROCESS!

FACT 2:   Parenting is not an easy job for the most part so when you kick it up a notch to a blended family, the word NO is important and EASY is absent from the equations.

FACT 3:   YOU have no legal rights to these children unless the children are adopted by you. We have included legal rights documentation for your review. As of this date of publication, the law is as stated. Please check with your state of residency for your rights and responsibilities awarded and not awarded to you as a stepparent.

FACT 4:   Also be advised the X of your significant other may be aware of this lack of law and attempt to use it against you and your new relationship. Understand that FACT 3 is not a stumbling block in your decision to become a stepparent nor should it prevent you from being a successful stepparent. However, we belief you should be aware of this factor and you should take it into consideration.

FACT 5:   The children should not have a choice in your mate. This is not a misprint. Jesus did not choose Joseph or Mary. His Father (God) did the selecting. Just KIR (Keeping it real)

FACT 6:   *"Do not share your dream with a non-dreamer; they may be a Dreamtaker" jrn*

FACT 7:   It will take time for your new blended family to begin to feel comfortable and function like a well-oiled machine that you both desire.

FACT 8:   ASK – (A)lways (S)eek (K)nowledge. jrn

Learn what your enemies' or your opponents' <u>weapons</u> are then super charge your Lethal Weapons.

FACT 9:   If you have set a standard for yourself, do not allow substandard behavior or people to have you change your standard.

FACT 10:   "Stand up for the right thing then watch the left fall down." jrn

FACT 11:   Communication is vital to the survival of your relationship with the co-parent of your stepchildren. It will allow you both an opportunity to be aware.

FACT 12:   The benefit of fostering children over step parenting is that as a foster parent, you have rights with the children but as a stepparent, you have no or very limited rights.

FACT 13:   Do not give the opponent an opportunity to divide and conquer.

FACT 14:   Set up your stepchildren and your family up for success not failure!

FACT 15:   The biological parent of the stepchildren can only run one household and that is the one in which he or she is residing. The home of the X is just that the home of the X with the children.

FACT 16:   Accepting FACT 15 and recognizing when and where to draw the line is as simple as locating the threshold where issues occur.

FACT 17:   Do not expect more from a stepparent than you would expect from your X or yourself?

FACT 18:   If you allowed your children to run your relationship and it was failure, do not repeat this failure. The results will be the same!

FACT 19:   "Distractions keep you away from your Attractions" – jrn

FACT 20:   The words that you select to use will make a big difference in how you are heard, understood, misunderstood, appreciated, respected, disrespected, loved, disliked, desired, -this list can be as long as infinity. Words have an unbelievable important power in our lives.

Glossary

List of words, acronyms or phrases that have been defined in the book

Term	Definition	Source
Appreciation	1. gratitude; thankful recognition: They showed their appreciation by giving him a gold watch. 2. the act of estimating the qualities of things and giving them their proper value. 3. clear perception or recognition, especially of aesthetic quality: a course in art appreciation. 4. an increase or rise in the value of property, goods, etc. 5. critical notice; evaluation; opinion, as of a situation, person, etc. 6. a critique or written evaluation, especially when favorable.	Dictionary.com
Biological Parent	A parent who has conceived (biological mother) or sired (biological father) rather than adopted a child and whose genes are therefore transmitted to the child. Also called birth parent	Dictionary.com
Blended Family	A family that includes children from a previous relationship, marriage, divorce, separation by death, artificially inseminated birth	JRN
Blended Family	A family that includes children from a previous marriage of the wife, husband, or both parents	Merrian Dictionary
Chosen	Selected or marked for favor or special privilege <a chosen few>	
"Clown in every circus"	A phrase coined to use if and when the stepchildren or x factor presented unacceptable behavior or words	JRN
Co-parent	1. A divorced or separated parent who shares equally with the other parent in the custody and care of a child. 2. To share equally with another parent in the care of (a child). verb 3. To act as a co-parent.	Merrian Dictionary

Term	Definition	Source
Decision Making	The thought process of selecting a logical choice from the available options. When trying to make a good decision, a person must weigh the positives and negatives of each option, and consider all the alternatives. For effective decision making, a person must be able to forecast the outcome of each option as well, and based on all these items, determine which option is the best for that particular situation	Business Definition
Dream Maker	One who supports, encourages, and believes in the dream of a dreamer	JamArt
Dream Taker	One who takes a dream from a dreamer away via misunderstanding, misinterpretation or sabotage the dream and or the dreamer	JRN
Fire Drill	(1) An emergency action plan, which details what to do when a fire occurs (2) A fire prevention plan, which describes what to do to prevent a fire from occurring.	2001 National Fire Protection Association
Fire Drill	A readiness plan of words or actions practiced to control a negative response or action	JRN
Foresight	The ability to predict or the action of predicting what will happen or be needed in the future.	The Free Dictionary by Farlex
Heart of the Fruit	The seed implanted in the heart to produce a good or bad fruit	JRN
Hindsight 20 -20	Perfect understanding of an event after it has happened; - a term usually used with sarcasm in response to criticism of one's decision, implying that the critic is unfairly judging the wisdom of the decision in light of information that was not available when the decision was made.	The Free Dictionary by Farlex
IOW	Acronym for In other Words	Lethal Weapon
KIR	Keeping it real	Lethal Weapon
Leftovers	The overflow of a miracle, the entrée prepared from the remains of a previous meal, or the gift of renewed man or woman that has left a bad relationship and has upgraded his or her attitude, aspiration and drive to improvement.	JRN

Term	Definition	Source
Leftovers	Food that has not been finished at a meal and that is often served at another meal; a thing that remains after something is finished or ended	Merriam Dictionary
Metamorphosis	1. A complete change of physical form or substance 2. A complete change of character, appearance, etc. 3. A person or thing that has undergone metamorphosis 4. (zoology) the rapid transformation of a larva into an adult that occurs in certain animals, for example the stage between tadpole and frog or between chrysalis and butterfly	English Dictionary
Method to the Madness	The phrase is defined often as a plan behind a person's apparently inexplicable (unexplainable) behavior.	Dictionary.com
Ounce Touch	A personalized stylized greeting of recognition, that consists of the touching of different assigned digits between two people	AKBS Artimio Blackburn Sr.
Package Deal	A collection or group related goods or services sold as a unit. (Not people). A term used to describe a well-shaped woman.	Merriam Dictionary
Pawn	2. A person or an entity used to further the purposes of another	The Free Dictionary by Farlex
Pawn	Abbr. P Games - A chess piece of lowest value that may move forward one square at a time or two squares in the first move, capture other pieces only on a one-space diagonal forward move, and be promoted to any piece other than a king upon reaching the eighth rank.	The Free Dictionary by Farlex
Pound Shake	The pound hug (also referred to as a pound shake, hip-hop hug, one-armed hug, dude hug, cootie hug, homie hug, shug, hetero hug, bro-grab, bro hug, brah hug, thug hug, man-hug, or a daps) is a stylized greeting, exclusively performed between two people, that consists of a combination of a handshake and one-armed hug.	Wikipedia
Process	A series of actions or steps taken in order to achieve a particular end.	Webster's Online Dictionary

Term	Definition	Source
Rules of Engagement (ROE)	Are rules or directives to military forces (including individuals) that define the circumstances, conditions, degree, and manner in which the use of force, or actions which might be construed as provocative, may be applied.[1] They provide authorization for and/or limits on, among other things, the use of force and the employment of certain specific capabilities.	NATO MC 362/1
Set	The word that is noted or having the longest definition in the dictionary	Businessinsider.com
Smoothie Beverage	A thick beverage made from blended raw fruit and/or vegetables, with other ingredients such as water, ice, dairy products or sweeteners	Wikipedia
Stepparent	The spouse of a parent, who becomes the stepparent of that parent's children upon marriage. Stepparents are not legal parents of their spouse's children unless they complete a stepparent adoption, which requires the consent of the other legal parent or the termination of that parent's rights.	English Law Dictionary
Stepparent	Non-blood related parent to children of divorce, death or abandonment for reference in this book	JRN
Word	1 : something that is said b plural (1) : talk, discourse <putting one's feelings into words> (2) : the text of a vocal musical composition c : a brief remark or conversation <would like to have a word with you> 2a (1) : a speech sound or series of speech sounds that symbolizes and communicates a meaning usually without being divisible into smaller units capable of independent use (2) : the entire set of linguistic forms produced by combining a single base with various inflectional elements without change in the part of speech elements b (1) : a written or printed character or combination of characters representing a spoken word <the number of words to a line> — sometimes used with the first letter of a real or pretended taboo word prefixed as an often humorous euphemism <the first man to utter the f word on British TV — Time> <we were not afraid to use the d word and talk about death — Erma Bombeck> (2) : any segment of written or printed discourse ordinarily appearing between spaces or	www2.merriam-webster.com

Term	Definition	Source
	between a space and a punctuation mark c : a number of bytes processed as a unit and conveying a quantum of information in communication and computer work 3: order, command <don't move till I give the word> 4often capitalized a : logos b : gospel 1a c : the expressed or manifested mind and will of God 5a : news, information <sent word that he would be late> b : rumor 6: the act of speaking or of making verbal communication 7: saying, proverb 8: promise, declaration <kept her word> 9: a quarrelsome utterance or conversation —usually used in plural <they had words and parted> 10: a verbal signal : password 11slang —used interjectionally to express agreement — good word 1: a favorable statement <put in a good word for me> 2: good news <what's the good word> — in a word : in short — in so any words 1: in exactly those terms <implied that such actions were criminal but did not say so in so many words> 2: in plain forthright language <in so many words, she wasn't fit to be seen — Jean Stafford> — of few words : not inclined to say more than is necessary : laconic <a man of few words> — of one's word : that can be relied on to keep a promise —used only after man or woman <a man of his word>— upon my word : with my assurance : indeed	
X-Factor	A term that will be used to describe the divorced partner, the separated parent or the parent left behind the past relationship behavior, actions or reactions	

Bible Text and Stories

The History of Stepparents, Joseph the Stepparent

Bible Reference (KJV): Matthew 1:18-25

18 This is how the birth of Jesus Christ came about: His mother Mary was pledged to be married to Joseph, but before they came together, she was found to be with child through the Holy Spirit.

19 Because Joseph her husband was a righteous man and did not want to expose her to public disgrace, he had in mind to divorce her quietly.

20 But after he had considered this, an angel of the Lord appeared to him in a dream and said, "Joseph son of David, do not be afraid to take Mary home as your wife, because what is conceived in her is from the Holy Spirit.

21 She will give birth to a son, and you are to give him the name Jesus, because he will save his people from their sins."

22 All this took place to fulfill what the Lord had said through the prophet:

23 "The virgin will be with child and will give birth to a son, and they will call him Immanuel"-- which means, "God with us."

24 When Joseph awoke, he did what the angel of the Lord had commanded him and took Mary home as his wife.

25 But he had no union with her until she gave birth to a son. And he gave him the name Jesus.

Dreamtaker, Joseph the Dreamer

Bible Reference (KJV): Genesis 17:1-36

1 And Jacob dwelt in the land wherein his father was a stranger, in the land of Canaan.

2 These are the generations of Jacob. Joseph, being seventeen years old, was feeding the flock with his brethren; and the lad was with the sons of Bilhah, and with the sons of Zilpah, his father's wives: and Joseph brought unto his father their evil report.

3 Now Israel loved Joseph more than all his children, because he was the son of his old age: and he made him a coat of many colours.

4 And when his brethren saw that their father loved him more than all his brethren, they hated him, and could not speak peaceably unto him.

5 And Joseph dreamed a dream, and he told it his brethren: and they hated him yet the more.

6 And he said unto them, Hear, I pray you, this dream which I have dreamed:

7 For, behold, we were binding sheaves in the field, and, lo, my sheaf arose, and also stood upright; and, behold, your sheaves stood round about, and made obeisance to my sheaf.

8 And his brethren said to him, Shalt thou indeed reign over us? or shalt thou indeed have dominion over us? And they hated him yet the more for his dreams, and for his words.

9 And he dreamed yet another dream, and told it his brethren, and said, Behold, I have dreamed a dream more; and, behold, the sun and the moon and the eleven stars made obeisance to me.

10 And he told it to his father, and to his brethren: and his father rebuked him, and said unto him, What is this dream that thou hast dreamed? Shall I and thy mother and thy brethren indeed come to bow down ourselves to thee to the earth?

11 And his brethren envied him; but his father observed the saying.

12 And his brethren went to feed their father's flock in Shechem.

13 And Israel said unto Joseph, Do not thy brethren feed the flock in Shechem? come, and I will send thee unto them. And he said to him, Here am I.

14 And he said to him, Go, I pray thee, see whether it be well with thy brethren, and well with the flocks; and bring me word again. So he sent him out of the vale of Hebron, and he came to Shechem.

15 And a certain man found him, and, behold, he was wandering in the field: and the man asked him, saying, What seekest thou?

16 And he said, I seek my brethren: tell me, I pray thee, where they feed their flocks.

17 And the man said, They are departed hence; for I heard them say, Let us go to Dothan. And Joseph went after his brethren, and found them in Dothan.

18 And when they saw him afar off, even before he came near unto them, they conspired against him to slay him.

19 And they said one to another, Behold, **this dreamer** cometh.

20 Come now therefore, and let us slay him, and cast him into some pit, and we will say, Some evil beast hath devoured him: and we shall see what will become of his dreams.

21 And Reuben heard it, and he delivered him out of their hands; and said, Let us not kill him.

22 And Reuben said unto them, Shed no blood, **but cast him into this pit that is in the wilderness**, and lay no hand upon him; that he might rid him out of their hands, to deliver him to his father again.

23 And it came to pass, when Joseph was come unto his brethren, that they stript Joseph out of his coat, his coat of many colours that was on him;

24 And they took him, and cast him into a pit: and the pit was empty, there was no water in it.

25 And they sat down to eat bread: and they lifted up their eyes and looked, and, behold, a company of Ishmeelites came from Gilead with their camels bearing spicery and balm and myrrh, going to carry it down to Egypt.

26 And Judah said unto his brethren, What profit is it if we slay our brother, and conceal his blood?

27 Come, and let us sell him to the Ishmeelites, and let not our hand be upon him; for he is our brother and our flesh. And his brethren were content.

28 Then there passed by Midianites merchantmen; and they drew and lifted up Joseph out of the pit, and sold Joseph to the Ishmeelites for twenty pieces of silver: and they brought Joseph into Egypt.

29 And Reuben returned unto the pit; and, behold, Joseph was not in the pit; and he rent his clothes.

30 And he returned unto his brethren, and said, The child is not; and I, whither shall I go?

31 And they took Joseph's coat, and killed a kid of the goats, and dipped the coat in the blood;

32 And they sent the coat of many colours, and they brought it to their father; and said, This have we found: know now whether it be thy son's coat or no.

33 And he knew it, and said, It is my son's coat; an evil beast hath devoured him; Joseph is without doubt rent in pieces.

34 And Jacob rent his clothes, and put sackcloth upon his loins, and mourned for his son many days.

35 And all his sons and all his daughters rose up to comfort him; but he refused to be comforted; and he said, For I will go down into the grave unto my son mourning. Thus his father wept for him.

36 And the Midianites sold him into Egypt unto Potiphar, an officer of Pharaoh's, and captain of the guard.

Dreamtaker, Like Minded - Similar Situations

Bible Reference (NIV): Luke 1:39-45

39 At that time Mary got ready and hurried to a town in the hill country of Judea,

40 where she entered Zechariah's home and greeted Elizabeth.

41 When Elizabeth heard Mary's greeting, the baby leaped in her womb, and Elizabeth was filled with the Holy Spirit.

42 In a loud voice she exclaimed: "Blessed are you among women, and blessed is the child you will bear!

43 But why am I so favored, that the mother of my Lord should come to me?

44 As soon as the sound of your greeting reached my ears, the baby in my womb leaped for joy.

45 Blessed is she who has believed that the Lord would fulfill his promises to her!"

Leftovers, More than Enough

Bible Reference (NIV): Matthew 15:32-39

32 Jesus called his disciples to him and said, "I have compassion for these people; they have already been with me three days and have nothing to eat. I do not want to send them away hungry, or they may collapse on the way."

33 His disciples answered, "Where could we get enough bread in this remote place to feed such a crowd?"

34 "How many loaves do you have?" Jesus asked. "Seven," they replied, "and a few small fish."

35 He told the crowd to sit down on the ground.

36 Then he took the seven loaves and the fish, and when he had given thanks, he broke them and gave them to the disciples, and they in turn to the people.

37 They all ate and were satisfied. Afterward the disciples picked up seven basketful of broken pieces that were left over.

38 The number of those who ate was four thousand, besides women and children.

39 After Jesus had sent the crowd away, he got into the boat and went to the vicinity of Magadan."

Leftovers, From a Little to a Lot

Bible Reference (NIV): Matthew 12:30-44

30 And the apostles gathered themselves together unto Jesus, and told him all things, both what they had done, and what they had taught.

31 And he said unto them, Come ye yourselves apart into a desert place, and rest a while: for there were many coming and going, and they had no leisure so much as to eat.

32 And they departed into a desert place by ship privately.

33 And the people saw them departing, and many knew him, and ran afoot thither out of all cities, and outwent them, and came together unto him.

34 And Jesus, when he came out, saw much people, and was moved with compassion toward them, because they were as sheep not having a shepherd: and he began to teach them many things.

35 And when the day was now far spent, his disciples came unto him, and said, This is a desert place, and now the time is far passed:

36 Send them away, that they may go into the country round about, and into the villages, and buy themselves bread: for they have nothing to eat.

37 He answered and said unto them, Give ye them to eat. And they say unto him, Shall we go and buy two hundred pennyworth of bread, and give them to eat?

38 He saith unto them, How many loaves have ye? go and see. And when they knew, they say, Five, and two fishes.

39 And he commanded them to make all sit down by companies upon the green grass.

40 And they sat down in ranks, by hundreds, and by fifties.

41 And when he had taken the five loaves and the two fishes, he looked up to heaven, and blessed, and brake the loaves, and gave them to his disciples to set before them; and the two fishes divided he among them all.

42 And they did all eat, and were filled.

43 And they took up twelve baskets full of the fragments, and of the fishes.

44 And they that did eat of the loaves were about five thousand men

House Rules, First House

Bible Reference (KJV): Genesis 2:8-9

8 And the LORD God planted a garden eastward in Eden; and there he put the man whom he had formed.

9 And out of the ground made the LORD God to grow every tree that is pleasant to the sight, and good for food; the tree of life also in the midst of the garden, and the tree of knowledge of good and evil.

House Rules, First House Rule

Bible Reference (KJV): Genesis 2:16

16 And the LORD God commanded the man, saying, of every tree of the garden thou mayest freely eat:
17 But of the tree of the knowledge of good and evil, thou shalt not eat of it: for in the day that thou eatest thereof thou shalt surely die.

The Beginning, The Plan

Bible Reference (KJV): Genesis 18

1 The Lord appeared to Abraham near the great trees of Mamre while he was sitting at the entrance to his tent in the heat of the day.
2 Abraham looked up and saw three men standing nearby. When he saw them, he hurried from the entrance of his tent to meet them and bowed low to the ground.
3 He said, "If I have found favor in your eyes, my lord,a do not pass your servant by.
4 Let a little water be brought, and then you may all wash your feet and rest under this tree.
5 Let me get you something to eat, so you can be refreshed and then go on your way—now that you have come to your servant. "Very well," they answered, "do as you say."
6 So Abraham hurried into the tent to Sarah. "Quick," he said, "get three seahsb of the finest flour and knead it and bake some bread."
7 Then he ran to the herd and selected a choice, tender calf and gave it to a servant, who hurried to prepare it.
8 He then brought some curds and milk and the calf that had been prepared, and set these before them. While they ate, he stood near them under a tree.
9 "Where is your wife Sarah?" they asked him. "There, in the tent," he said.
10 Then one of them said, "I will surely return to you about this time next year, and Sarah your wife will have a son." Now Sarah was listening at the entrance to the tent, which was behind him.
11 Abraham and Sarah were already very old, and Sarah was past the age of childbearing.
12 So Sarah laughed to herself as she thought, "After I am worn out and my lord is old, will I now have this pleasure?"
13 Then the Lord said to Abraham, "Why did Sarah laugh and say, 'Will I really have a child, now that I am old?'
14 Is anything too hard for the Lord? I will return to you at the appointed time next year, and Sarah will have a son."
15 Sarah was afraid, so she lied and said, "I did not laugh." But he said, "Yes, you did laugh."

The Beginning, The Surrogate Mother

Bible Reference (KJV): Genesis 16:1-4

1 Now Sarai Abram's wife bare him no children: and she had an handmaid, an Egyptian, whose name was Hagar.
2 And Sarai said unto Abram, Behold now, the Lord hath restrained me from bearing: I pray thee, go in unto my maid; it may be that I may obtain children by her. And Abram hearkened to the voice of Sarai.
3 And Sarai Abram's wife took Hagar her maid the Egyptian, after Abram had dwelt ten years in the land of Canaan, and gave her to her husband Abram to be his wife.
4 And he went in unto Hagar, and she conceived: and when she saw that she had conceived, her mistress was despised in her eyes.

The Beginning, Being Obedient

Bible Reference (KJV): Genesis 21

1 Now the Lord was gracious to Sarah as he had said, and the Lord did for Sarah what he had promised.

2 Sarah became pregnant and bore a son to Abraham in his old age, at the very time God had promised him.

3 Abraham gave the name Isaac to the son Sarah bore him.

4 When his son Isaac was eight days old, Abraham circumcised him, as God commanded him.

5 Abraham was a hundred years old when his son Isaac was born to him.

6 Sarah said, "God has brought me laughter, and everyone who hears about this will laugh with me."

7 And she added, "Who would have said to Abraham that Sarah would nurse children? Yet I have borne him a son in his old age." Hagar and Ishmael Sent Away

8 The child grew and was weaned, and on the day Isaac was weaned Abraham held a great feast.

9 But Sarah saw that the son whom Hagar the Egyptian had borne to Abraham was mocking,

10 and she said to Abraham, "Get rid of that slave woman and her son, for that woman's son will never share in the inheritance with my son Isaac."

11 The matter distressed Abraham greatly because it concerned his son.

12 But God said to him, "Do not be so distressed about the boy and your slave woman. Listen to whatever Sarah tells you, because it is through Isaac that your offspring will be reckoned.

13 I will make the son of the slave into a nation also, because he is your offspring."

14 Early the next morning Abraham took some food and a skin of water and gave them to Hagar. He set them on her shoulders and then sent her off with the boy. She went on her way and wandered in the Desert of Beersheba.

15 When the water in the skin was gone, she put the boy under one of the bushes.

16 Then she went off and sat down about a bowshot away, for she thought, "I cannot watch the boy die." And as she sat there, she began to sob.

17 God heard the boy crying, and the angel of God called to Hagar from heaven and said to her, "What is the matter, Hagar? Do not be afraid; God has heard the boy crying as he lies there.

18 Lift the boy up and take him by the hand, for I will make him into a great nation."

19 Then God opened her eyes and she saw a well of water. So she went and filled the skin with water and gave the boy a drink.

20 God was with the boy as he grew up. He lived in the desert and became an archer.

21 While he was living in the Desert of Paran, his mother got a wife for him from Egypt.

Back to the Basics, Children Brings their Own Drama

Bible Reference (KJV): Genesis 4:1-12

1 Now Adam knew Eve his wife, and she conceived and bore Cain, and said, "I have acquired a man from the Lord."

2 Then she bore again, this time his brother Abel. Now Abel was a keeper of sheep, but Cain was a tiller of the ground.

3 And in the process of time it came to pass that Cain brought an offering of the fruit of the ground to the Lord.

4 Abel also brought of the firstborn of his flock and of their fat. And the Lord respected Abel and his offering,

5 but He did not respect Cain and his offering. And Cain was very angry, and his countenance fell.

6 So the Lord said to Cain, "Why are you angry? And why has your countenance fallen?

7 If you do well, will you not be accepted? And if you do not do well, sin lies at the door. And its desire is for you, but you should rule over it."

8 Now Cain talked with Abel his brother;[a] and it came to pass, when they were in the field, that Cain rose up against Abel his brother and killed him.

9 Then the Lord said to Cain, "Where is Abel your brother?" He said, "I do not know. Am I my brother's keeper?"

10 And He said, "What have you done? The voice of your brother's blood cries out to Me from the ground.

11 So now you are cursed from the earth, which has opened its mouth to receive your brother's blood from your hand.

12 When you till the ground, it shall no longer yield its strength to you. A fugitive and a vagabond you shall be on the earth."

The Heart of the Fruit, What's in the Heart

Bible Reference (KJV): Luke 6:45

A good man out of the good treasure of his heart bringeth forth that which is good; and an evil man out of the evil treasure of his heart bringeth forth that which is evil: for of the abundance of the heart his mouth speaketh."

Leftovers, Peter Moment

Bible Reference (KJV): Matthew 16:13-23

13 When Jesus came into the coasts of Caesarea Philippi, he asked his disciples, saying, Whom do men say that I the Son of man am?

14 And they said, Some say that thou art John the Baptist: some, Elias; and others, Jeremias, or one of the prophets.

15 He saith unto them, But whom say ye that I am?

16 And Simon Peter answered and said, Thou art the Christ, the Son of the living God.

17 And Jesus answered and said unto him, Blessed art thou, Simon Barjona: for flesh and blood hath not revealed it unto thee, but my Father which is in heaven.

18 And I say also unto thee, That thou art Peter, and upon this rock I will build my church; and the gates of hell shall not prevail against it.

19 And I will give unto thee the keys of the kingdom of heaven: and whatsoever thou shalt bind on earth shall be bound in heaven: and whatsoever thou shalt loose on earth shall be loosed in heaven.

20 Then charged he his disciples that they should tell no man that he was Jesus the Christ.

21 From that time forth began Jesus to shew unto his disciples, how that he must go unto Jerusalem, and suffer many things of the elders and chief priests and scribes, and be killed, and be raised again the third day.

22 Then Peter took him, and began to rebuke him, saying, Be it far from thee, Lord: this shall not be unto thee.

23 But he turned, and said unto Peter, Get thee behind me, Satan: thou art an offence unto me: for thou savourest not the things that be of God, but those that be of men.

Closing Thoughts, Power of Words

Bible Reference (KJV): Genesis 1:3, 6

3 And God said, Let there be light: and there was light.

6 And God said, Let there be a firmament in the midst of the waters, and let it divide the waters from the waters.

Closing Thoughts, Influence of Words

Bible Reference (KJV): Proverbs 18:21

21 Death and life are in the power of the tongue: and they that love it shall eat the fruit thereof.

Closing Thoughts, Impact of "Word"

Bible Reference (KJV): John 1:1:2

1 In the beginning was the Word, and the Word was with God, and the Word was God.
2 The same was in the beginning with God

Lethal Weapon – Companion Workbook

Jamera Napier and Artimio Blackburn Sr

Table of Contents

Some Thoughts to Consider

"The most important relationship to nurture in any stepfamily is between the adult partners" says experts in the field. In fact, putting more energy and effort into coupledom may improve your relationships with all the children, extended family, friends and relationships who will begin to see you as a strong, united front instead of two bewildered (or even squabbling) individuals.

To accomplish this goal, you need to set aside time alone with your partner to discuss family issues. At each meeting, pick the two most important problems then brainstorm solutions. At the end of each meeting, do something special together for example:

- Go out and get a great cup of coffee, tea or your choice of beverage
- Plan some intimate time with your mate,
- Think of your best intimate act, discuss it, and then see what happens next.
- Watch a movie sitting or lying together.
- Schedule date nights and weekends away when kid-related topics are off limits.

We all know that planning, scheduling, and communicating can be adventurous but worth it, say professionals in the field and us, that learning from past relationship mistakes makes couples in stepfamilies better able to weather family storms. We are hopeful that this workbook will assist in helping you both to be in a position to bypass the hard way of learning life's lessons and find yourselves knocking a grand slam as you blend a successful family.

Lethal Weapon Companion book is a tool to assist you in tightening your nuts and bolts of understanding of you and your new chosen mate, understanding of the floor plan you will need to establish in order to build your successful blended family home, and written encouragement that you, too, can be a successful couple with the added features of a good successful blended family.

Due to the very sensitive nature of this subject matter, we recommend that each question and topic is approached with loving caution. This workbook is not designed to be treated like a fast food meal. This workbook is living document wherein we encourage you to approach its contents and application like a 7 course 5 star meal that will be hand prepared to your individual specifications.

In other words, this is not a workbook that has a solution in the back of the book. How fast you are able to complete determines your readiness. This book is designed to be completed in bite-sized nibbles.

The correct answers will be the compromise of the agreement of understanding that you and your mate establish to create your desired blended family.

This workbook is designed to be a road map to assist in preparing you and your mate for journey of concerns that we believe need to be addressed if you are to successfully take the step out of step parenting.

How to Use LW Companion Workbook

Lethal Weapon Training Companion

Workbook by definition is a booklet containing problems, questions, and or exercises with space included for written answers.

Companion by definition is one of a pair of things intended to complement or match each other. (Like peanut butter and jelly; salad and dressings, meat and potatoes)

The 10 steps listed below are to be taken into consideration, not over estimating the challenge that will be required to successfully reach your desired outcome:

Step 1 **Step up** … To the challenge to commit the time, patience, understanding, and honesty to each question or scenario listed in this workbook and your undivided attention plus your diligence to be successful.

Step 2 **Step Down** … On your anger, frustrations, disappointments, lack of understanding met and unmet expectations.

Step 3 **Step Closer** … To your chosen stepparent and or co-parent to showing you care more than enough to do whatever it takes to successfully take the step out of step parenting.

Step 4 **Step Away** … From any interruptions, interference or distractions that may prevent you from successfully completing step one. (Cell phones, tablets, games, computers, TV, radio, barking dogs, children, email, texting, and even your co parent until it is time to share answers to reach a common ground of understanding.)

Step 5 **Step Back** … To the main of objective of your relationship to love each other first and foremost. You both decided that you would love each other more than enough that you wanted to blend his or her family to your loving relationship.

Step 6 **Step Over** … Into another level of understanding that it may take more than one discussion before both parties agree to a standard of operating procedures on how to resolve issues or current conflict.

Step 7 **Step Toward** … A better understanding of your mate's response, lack of response, action or lack of action.

Step 8 **Step Beside** … Your mate in giving them the one gift that is second to love – attention.

Step 9 **Step Forward** … In the fact that these steps may be the first steps you take toward ensuring the security of your relationship and successful steps to blending your family.

Step 10 **Step Into** … The shoes of the emotions, feelings, hurt, pain, anguish, understanding, lack of understanding, fear, disrespect, lack of appreciation, lack of gratitude of your chosen partner.

(The book, <u>Lethal Weapon – Taking the Step out of Step Parenting,</u> will give you more steps on how to achieve this goal.)

Prepare for Discussion

☐ Share your responses with no one prior to your mate. This act alone will allow you and your mate to have an honest heart to heart conversation with outside interference.

☐ Time – (allow yourself a minimum of 7 minutes per question or scenario).

☐ Why 7 minutes? We share the meaning of the number 7.

☐ Writing tool or recording tool (smart phone voice record).

☐ Writing notebook or electronic notebook. (Tablet or computer).

☐ Choose 3-5 questions from the companion – workbook.

☐ Think about the question and what you think it is asking you.

☐ Record your answer in a notebook, journal, and a paper napkin if necessary.

> By writing or recording your responses, this may relieve the burden of worrying about whether or not you will remember your responses when you need to share the answer with your mate. This record may also be used as a reminder of responses or suggested actions to be taken.

☐ Read questions very carefully.

☐ If the listed question brings to your mind another question that you believe to appropriate then record it. Share this new question with your mate and remember to allow your mate time to address the question.

☐ Unless directed to do otherwise, answer the easier questions first.

☐ Read each question twice to be sure you completely understand it before answering.

☐ Write legibly or record in a quiet zone.

☐ Review your answer.

☐ Wait for scheduled time to discuss responses with your mate. Timing is very important!

☐ Listen! This step is very important: Do you really know the artful skill of listening? We thought we knew until we learned better. To know better is to do better. How to listen will be shared in section 3 of this workbook.

The Meaning of Numbers: The Number 7 www.biblestudy.org

Seven is the number of completeness and perfection (both physical and spiritual). It derives much of its meaning from being tied directly to God's creation of all things.

According to Jewish tradition, the creation of Adam occurred on October 7th, 3761 B.C. (or the first day of Tishri, which is the seventh month on the Hebrew calendar).

The word 'created' is used 7 times describing God's creative work (Genesis 1:1, 21, 27 three times; 2:3; 2:4).

There are 7 days in a week and God's Sabbath is on the 7th day.

The Bible, as a whole, was originally divided into 7 major divisions. They are 1) the Law; 2) the Prophets; 3) the Writings, or Psalms; 4) the Gospels and Acts; 5) the General Epistles; 6) the Epistles of Paul; and 7) the book of Revelation.

The total number of originally inspired books was forty-nine, or 7 x 7, demonstrating the absolute perfection of the Word of God.

The Numerology Meaning of the Number 7

Positive Characteristics: 7 isn't just a lucky number. It's also spiritual, intelligent, analytical, focused, introspective, studious, intuitive, knowledgeable, contemplative, serious, persevering, refined, gracious and displays much inner wisdom. (www.numerology.com)

Symbolism of the number 7 (www.ridingthebeast.com)

- The seven indicates the senses of a change after an accomplished cycle and of a positive renewal.
- Symbol of the totality of the created Universe (3 the sky + 4 the earth), it expresses the creation within which the man evolves.
- Saint Augustin sees the seven like the perfection of the Plenitude. He made it also the number of the creature, considering not the life of this one but it become, the evolution.
- Symbol of the infinite numbered in its return to the principle, that of the snake which bites its tail, according to Abellio. It would be also the number of the achievement in the space-time.
- It is the number of the initiation, that is to say the union of exhibited with the infinity.
- Symbol of eternal life for the Egyptians: it symbolizes a complete cycle, a dynamic perfection.

- For the Indians in the prairie and the "Pueblo" Indians, the number seven represents the cosmic coordinate of the man.

- In Africa and for the Bambaras of Senegal, seven is a symbol of the perfection and the unity.

- The "Dogons" consider the number seven as the symbol of the union of the opposites, of the resolution of dualism, therefore like symbol of unity and perfection. It is also the mark of the master of the word.

  - The Pythagoreans call the number 7 "the Septad" (the unit of 7)

  - There are 7 colors in the rainbow (Red Orange Yellow Green Blue Indigo Violet)

  - There are seven notes in the diatonic scale (In music a scale composed of 7 pitch classes)

  - There are seven letters in the Roman numeral system (I V X L C D M)

- The seven symbolizes the cross with its six directions plus the center - indefinite extents moving toward the top, the bottom, the right, the left, forwards and backwards.

- The dice symbolizes the seven: the dice itself, 1, having 6 faces.

- QWERTY Keyboard #7 share the "&" sign. Hold the shift key and you get the "and" (Complete you & your new mate by simply holding the compromise shifts of agreement on the how, why, where, when, and what you both will do to become another successful loving couple and a successful blended family)

•

How to Listen

I always say "God gave us 2 ears and only one mouth. That should tell you something" jrn

Listening is the ability to accurately receive and interpret messages in the communication process.

Listening is key to all effective communication, without the ability to listen effectively messages are easily misunderstood – communication breaks down and the sender of the message can easily become frustrated or irritated.

Listening is so important that many top employers provide listening skills training for their employees. This is not surprising when you consider that good listening skills can lead to: better customer satisfaction, greater productivity with fewer mistakes, increased sharing of information that in turn can lead to more creative and innovative work. (In this case:-successful relationship and successfully blended families.)

Effective listening is a skill that underpins all positive human relationships. Spend some time thinking about and developing your listening skills – they are the building blocks of success.

Good listening skills also have benefits in our personal lives, including:

A greater number of friends and social networks, improved self-esteem and confidence, higher grades at school and in academic work and even better health and general wellbeing. Studies have shown that, whereas speaking raises blood pressure, listening brings it down.

Listening is not the same as Hearing

Hearing refers to the sounds that you hear, whereas listening requires more than that: it requires focus. Listening means paying attention not only to the story, but how it is told, the use of language and voice, and how the other person uses his or her body. In other words, it means being aware of both verbal and non-verbal messages. Your ability to listen effectively depends on the degree to which you perceive and understand these messages.

We Spend a Lot of Time Listening

Adults spend an average of 70% of their time engaged in some sort of communication, of this an average of 45% is spent listening compared to 30% speaking, 16% reading and 9% writing. (Adler, R. et al. 2001).

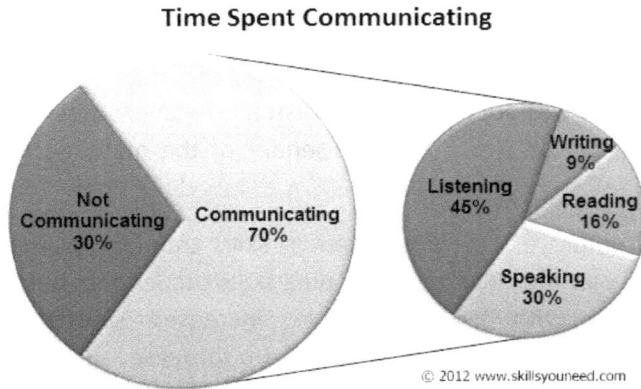

Time Spent Communicating

© 2012 www.skillsyouneed.com

Based on the research of: *Adler, R., Rosenfeld, L. and Proctor, R. (2001) Interplay: the process of interpersonal communicating (8th edn), Fort Worth, TX: Harcourt.*

Effective listening requires concentration and the use of your other senses - not just hearing the words spoken.

Listening is not the same as hearing and in order to listen effectively you need to use more than just your ears.

The 10 Principles of Listening

A good listener will listen not only to what is being said, but also to what is left unsaid or only partially said.

Effective listening involves observing body language and noticing inconsistencies between verbal and non-verbal messages.

For example: If someone tells you that they are happy with their life but through gritted teeth or with tears filling their eyes, you should consider that the verbal and non-verbal messages are in conflict; they maybe don't mean what they say.

01 Stop Talking

Don't talk. Listen. When somebody else is talking, listen to what they are saying. Do not interrupt, talk over them or finish their sentences for them. Stop. Just listen. When the other person has finished talking, you may need to clarify to ensure you have received their message accurately.

02 Prepare Yourself to Listen

Relax.

Focus on the speaker. Put other things out of mind. The human mind is easily distracted by other thoughts – what's for lunch, what time do I need to leave to catch my train, is it going to rain – try to put other thoughts out of mind and concentrate on the messages that are being communicated.

03 Put the Speaker at Ease

Help the speaker to feel free to speak.

Remember their needs and concerns. Nod or use other gestures or words to encourage them to continue.

Maintain eye contact but don't stare – show you are listening and understand what is being said.

04 Remove Distractions

Focus on what is being said.

Don't doodle, shuffle papers, look out the window, pick your fingernails or similar. Avoid unnecessary interruptions. These behaviors disrupt the listening process and send messages to the speaker that you are bored or distracted.

05 Empathize

Try to understand the other person's point of view.

Look at issues from their perspective. Let go of preconceived ideas. By having an open mind, we can more fully empathize with the speaker. If the speaker says something that you disagree with, then wait and construct an argument to counter what is said but keep an open mind to the views and opinions of others.

06 Be Patient

A pause, even a long pause, does not necessarily mean that the speaker has finished.

Be patient and let the speaker continue in their own time, sometimes it takes time to formulate what to say and how to say it. Never interrupt or finish a sentence for someone.

07 Avoid Personal Prejudice

Try to be impartial.

Don't become irritated and don't let the person's habits or mannerisms distract you from what the speaker is really saying. Everybody has a different way of speaking - some people are for example more nervous or shy than others, some have regional accents or make excessive arm movements, some people like to pace while talking - others like to sit still. Focus on what is being said and try to ignore styles of delivery.

08 Listen to the Tone

Volume and tone both add to what someone is saying.

A good speaker will use both volume and tone to their advantage to keep an audience attentive; everybody will use pitch, tone and volume of voice in certain situations – let these help you to understand the emphasis of what is being said.

09 Listen for Ideas – Not Just Words

You need to get the whole picture, not just isolated bits and pieces.

Maybe one of the most difficult aspects of listening is the ability to link together pieces of information to reveal the ideas of others. With proper concentration, letting go of distractions, and focus this becomes easier.

10 Wait and Watch for Non-Verbal Communication

Gestures, facial expressions, and eye-movements can all be important.

Find more at: http://www.skillsyouneed.com/ips/listening-skills.html

Fact Sheet

List of all of the FACTS denoted in the book:

FACT 1: Surviving step parenting successfully will be a PROCESS!

FACT 2: Parenting is <u>no easy</u> job for the most part so when you kick it up a notch to a blended family, the word NO is important and EASY is absent from the equations.

FACT 3: YOU have no legal rights to these children unless the children are adopted by you. We have included legal rights documentation for your review. As of this date of publication, the law is as stated. Please check with your state of residence for your rights and responsibilities awarded and not awarded to you as a stepparent.

FACT 4: Also be advised the X of your significant other may be aware of this law and attempt to use it against you and your new relationship. Understand that FACT 3 is not a stumbling block in your decision to become a stepparent nor should it prevent you from being a successful stepparent. However, it is a factor that we have supplied some support documentation in the index of this book.

FACT 5: The children should not have a choice in your mate. This is not a misprint and we will discuss in later chapter. Jesus did not chose Joseph or Mary. His Father did the preferred selecting. Just KIR (keeping it real)

FACT 6: Do not share your dreams with non-dreamers.

FACT 7: It will take time for your new blended family to begin to feel comfortable and function like a well-oiled machine that you both desire.

FACT 8: ASK – (A)lways (S)eek (K)nowledge. jrn

Learn what your enemies or your opponents' weapon are then super charge your Lethal Weapons.

FACT 9: If you have set a standard for yourself, do not allow substandard behavior or people to have you change your standard.

FACT 10: "Stand up for the right thing then watch the left fall down." jrn

FACT 11:   Communication is vital to the survival of your relationship with the Parent of your stepchildren. It will allow you both an opportunity to be aware.

FACT 12:   The benefit of fostering children over step parenting is that as a foster parent, you have rights with the children, but as a stepparent, you have no or very limited rights.

FACT 13:   Do not give the opponent an opportunity to divide and conquer

FACT 14:   Set up your stepchildren and your family up for success not failure!

FACT 15:   The biological parent of the stepchildren can only run one household and that is the one in which he or she is residing. The home of the X is just that the home of the X with the children.

FACT 16:   Accepting FACT 15 and recognizing when and where to draw the line is as simply as locating the threshold where issues occur.

FACT 17:   Do not expect more from a stepparent than you would expect from your X or yourself?

FACT 18:   If you allowed your children to run your relationship and it was a failure, do not repeat failures. The results will be the same!

FACT 19:   "Distractions keep you away from your Attractions" – jrn

FACT 20:   The words that you select to use will make a big difference in how you are heard, understood, misunderstand, appreciated, respected, disrespected, loved, disliked, desired, -this list can be as long as infinity. Words have an unbelievable important power in our lives.

ABC of Step Parenting – Inspiration

A	Attitude
B	Behavior
C	Communications & Control
D	Destroy the demons
E	Expect the Unexpected
F	Find workable solutions
G	Guarded our ultimate goals
H	Help each other pass the rough spots
I	Important before Injustice
J	Jump behind each in support
K	Kept sight
L	On our love
M	On our mission
N	*"No"* and *"not acceptable"* became apart mantra
O	Opposed our Haters
P	Proactive planning
Q	Quit living in Fear
R	Respect was not a request
S	Set Standards
T	Together we stood
U	Unified our purpose
V	Victory was our prayer
W	Winning was our only option
X	X understood:
Y	Wh(y) he or she was not in control of our lives
Z	"Zip out the bad behavior and zip up the good" jrn

This list was very influential for us and we welcome the opportunity for you to introduce, practice and help this list to grow with back to the basic practice to assist this important behind the scene role of step parenting.

"Perfect Practice makes Perfection" JRN

120 Questions for Discussion

1. How did you become a stepparent?

   _____

2. Why would you or have you taken on the challenge of being a stepparent?

   _____

3. What is your personal knowledge or relationship to step parenting or stepchildren?

   _____

4. Are your experiences related to step parenting or stepchildren positive or negative?

   _____

5. What is your most positive step parenting experience shared, heard about or witnessed?

   _____

6. What is your most negative step parenting experience shared, heard about or witnessed?

   _____

7. What do you think could have changed the outcome of the previous question?

   _____

8. Are you prepared to be a parent to a child that does not have your DNA?

   _____

9. What steps have you taken to become prepared for your role as a stepparent?

   _____

10. What steps have you taken to prepare in your role as a co-parent with a stepparent?

    _____

11. How long are you willing to stay in this relationship?

    _____

12. How do you share your concerns about issues you may encounter as a stepparent?

    _____

13. Whom do you share your concerns about issues you may encounter as a stepparent?

    _____

14. Why this individual, group or agency is your choice to share your concerns?

    _____

15. What makes this person, group or individual qualified to hear and assisted in your issues?

    _____

16. What exactly does the term "Package deal" mean to you as it related to stepparents?

    _____

17. Does that mean take it or leave it for your new potential mate? In Other Words (**IOW**) – Take me with my children or leave me alone.

    _____

18. Does it mean that you have no options in this relationship? **IOW** – This is my final offer - me and them or no me!

_____

19. Does it mean that it is only a one-way street? **IOW** – It will be our way or no way!

_____

20. Does it mean you and yours have the right of passage and your new chosen mate is to be at a roadblock, detour, or a never-ending crossroad? **IOW** – Accept whatever we bring to the table however we bring it because we are hurting from divorce, separation and loss, so deal with it.

_____

21. What if your new chosen mate has children and now you both have package deals? **IOW** – Now what? Who wins the first chair--your kids or mine?

_____

22. How does this business deal work out? **IOW** – Win-Win, Win- Lose, Lose-Win or Lose-Lose

_____

23. Which one of the packages gets more of a deal of your time than the other? **IOW** – Choose one – the children out of the blended shared home or the children in the blended home.

_____

24. Which one of the packages gets left behind? **IOW** – Choose one – In the stepparent's house or custodial parent's house.

_____

25. Which one of the package gets moved forward in front of the other? **IOW** – Choose one – In the stepparent's house or custodial parent's house.

_____

26. How are the options and roadblocks determined? **IOW** – What steps are taken to measure what is best for the family?

_____

27. If your package is you and the children what role does the X Factor play? **IOW** – How much control will the X have in the blended home?

_____

28. What role will you being playing in this package? **IOW** – Hurt Father? Recovered Dad? Hurt Mom? Recovered Mom?

_____

29. What role do the children get to play? **IOW** – Masters of the relationship? Captain of the Ship? Child of Recovery?

_____

30. How long do the children get to play this role? **IOW** – Until healing begins? Until your relationship ends?

_____

31. How do you and I agree to the roles that are to be played? **IOW** – Uncle or Aunt? Ice Cream   Daddy?   Sugar   Coat   Mommy?

   _____

32. How do we stop the role of the X factor from destroying our new package?

   _____

33. If you are a package deal, what is the bonus prize or discount for your new mate?

   _____

34. When you and your new mate come to a crossroad in your decisions about the package, then   whom   do   you   go   to   try   to   get   resolution?

   _____

35. Referring to the co-parent – How do you bring this entire package to the table and have no   plans   for   success?

   _____

36. Referring to the stepparent – How do you accept this entire package and have no plans for success?

   _____

37. Where will you go to get the support, compassion or understanding when the packager is not   handling   his   or   her   package   on   your   behalf   or   benefit?

   _____

38. What happens when the packager is torn between their children's guilt, his or her guilt for the loss (separation, divorce or death) of the other biological parent and the stepparent?

   _____

39. Would   you   allow   your   children   to   rule   your   new   chosen   mate?

   _____

40. Would you allow children to run amok on your chosen guest, disrespect you, your parents, your employer, your employees, your friends, your neighbors, your pastor, or even your pet?

   _____

41. Are   you   willing   to   allow   your   children   to   become   the   ruler   over   you?

   _____

42. Would it be acceptable for your children to be disruptive, disrespectful and totally ignore the teachers or authority figures (well if it a policeman, the rules automatically change)?

   _____

43. Did your child ask you and your X to get a divorce so that the child can become ruler?

   _____

44. Did you and your X consult your children about the getting a divorce and whatever their decision   was   you   and   your   X   would   agree   to   those   terms?

   _____

45. Did you and your X inform your children that you were getting a divorce and they would take on the role as adult parents?

_____

46. The answers to the previously listed question regarding children controlling your relationship should be a majority of NO! And some maybe H*** NO! Do you agree or disagree.

_____

47. Where and how do these statements come into play in the big scheme of family, hierarchy and structure?

_____

48. Did you know that you do not have any legal rights to your stepchildren?

_____

49. Did you know, Stepparent, that you can obtain a medical release form to authorize you to be able to authorize medical treatment for a minor child?

_____

50. Did you know, Stepparent, that if you are cohabitating adults and you are not married by law, you can use a lease agreement to protect you from having to pay child support for your stepchildren?

_____

51. Did you know if you are granted the permission to add your stepchildren to your taxes because you cared financially for them that you should get a statement from the children's parents have it notarized to show proof if needed by the IRS?

_____

52. Did you know you could adopt your stepchildren? You will have to obtain permission from both biological parents.

_____

53. Did you know you have a right to have respect from your stepchildren?

_____

54. Are you stubborn in your current outlook?

_____

55. Are you aware of the body language, silence, written or oral communication from your mate that may express this list (Attitude, posture, pleased, not pleased, approval or disapproval? If so, identify?

_____

56. How important is your relationship with your chosen mate?

_____

57. Are you willing to allow your past life to stop or interfere with your new relationship? If not, Why not?

_____

58. Do you accept the idea that your children, your X, your friends, your family and acquaintance can fabricate and/ or stretch the truth?

_____

59. Do you think that your X spouse or X partners has the power of influence of you and your decisions?

_____

60. Are you willing to invest time into your new relationship to ensure a successfully blended family?

_____

61. Are you willing to compromise time, even if the time compromised will cause a loss of time with your children?

_____

62. Are you willing to set aside previous plans for a non-emergency situation that may arise with children (bio or step)? If so, how often? What determines if you will set aside previous plan for non-emergency?

_____

63. What are emergency situations with children or stepchildren?

_____

64. Do you have the ability to see problems beyond pre-existing behavior? I.e. oh the child did not mean to use profanity with you. That is just what the child does when he or she is angry.

_____

65. Do you know if your partner's has long and or short-term life dreams? If so, what are they? If not, why aren't you aware of your partner's dreams?

_____

66. Will his or her dreams be attainable with you? How can you help? What can you do that might cause harm?

_____

67. Do you have long or short-term life dreams? Is your mate aware of these dreams? If not, why not? Are your dreams attainable in this a relationship? If so, how? If not, Why?

_____

68. Are you willing to make sacrifices for the children, stepchildren or/ and stepparent?

_____

69. Are you willing to make sacrifices for the children, stepchildren or/and co-parent?

_____

70. What is the current response to stepchildren and X factor issues when they arise?

_____

71. What would be your ideal response to these types of issues?

_____

72. What role are you playing in the issues?

_____

73. How can you assist in defining a solution for stepchildren and X factor issues?

_____

74. Are you willing to comprise even if you believe your way is the best way?

_____

75. Can you list examples where there will be absolutely no compromise? Why?

_____

76. Can you separate stepparent and stepchildren issues from you and your new relationship? How can you identify separation? How can you begin separation? How will you evaluate if your actions of separation are effective?

_____

77. Are you capable of separating your work life from your home life?

_____

78. Can you separate your past mate's dislikes, likes, desires, from your current mate's likes, dislikes, desires etc.? (i.e., when my X cook for me and the kids, they did it this way and that is the way we want it.)

_____

79. Are you free to love without chains of guilt linked from your past relationships?

_____

80. How do you recover with your stepparent after stepchildren and/ or X factor issues?

_____

81. Are you willing to seek counseling or outside aides (like this book Lethal Weapon) to assist in developing your new or old blended family?

_____

82. Do you have a backup plan ready if this relationship fails? If so, why?

_____

83. Would you classify your personality as more positive or negative?

_____

84. Would your personality classification be the same answers as your mate's?

_____

85. Would you say your mate's personality is positive or negative as it relates to stepchildren or X factor issues? Why do you think your choice is a perfect choice?

_____

86. Are you the same person in your home as you are outside of your home? If so, how? If not, how? Why are you the same or different? Does your mate agree with this answer?

_____

87. List 7 great things that you are impressed with about your chosen mate?

_____

88. Are you willing to work to keep these 7 impressionable things alive and well in your relationship?

_____

89. Are any of these 7 great things changeable? If so, how? Do you think you or your issues with X factor or stepchildren are a factor?

_____

90. Are you seeking an adult to help you financially and raise your children or are you seeking someone to love you for you and you love them for them?

_____

91. Do you think your mate is just seeking an adult to help raise the children financially and you tolerate them for the benefits?

_____

92. Are you capable of recognizing when you are wrong? Are you willing to apologize?

_____

93. Are you forgiving in nature or act? Is your mate forgiving in nature or act?

_____

94. Is your mate capable of recognizing when they are wrong? Are they willing to apologize?

_____

95. Are you forgetful? Is your mate forgetful?

_____

96. Do you have selective memory that is "recall" when it is convenient?

_____

97. Does your chosen mate have selective memory?

_____

98. Do you recognize when you are in these emotional states (angry, frustrated, bothered, troubled or stressed? What are your signs or signals?

_____

99. Do you know if your chosen mate is aware of the signs or signals when you are angry, frustrated, bothered, troubled or stressed?

_____

100. Do you recognize when you are in these emotional states (happy, overjoyed, inspired, influenced, manipulated, hungry, exhausted, relieved, tolerated, etc.)? What are your signs or signals?

_____

101. What is the order of hierarchy in your blended family? Dad Mom Kids, Dad Kids Mom Kids Mom Dad or Kids Mom Dad? Why?

_____

102. If the roles were reversed from your answer, would you be comfortable in the same position? If so, why? If not, why?

_____

103. Are you family oriented?

_____

104. What are the similarities of you and your mate?

_____

105. Would your relationship survive if any changes were to occur to those similarities?

_____

106. Do you compliment your partner's strength's? If so, how?

_____

107. Do you value your current relationship?

_____

108. Do you believe your relationship can survive blending a family?

_____

109. What suggestions can you make to encourage survival?

_____

110. Do you know how your new chosen mate feels about the following: sex, money, religion, religious practices, saving, work, risk, sleep, health, exercise, children, X factor, opposite sex and you, food, time alone, time shared, cleanliness, vacations, time, living accommodations, friends, and family?

_____

111. Do you have any favorite personal items or tokens that you would be heartbroken if damaged or broken? If so, can you identify them? Do you know if your mate is aware of these special tokens?

_____

112. Do you have a best time for you to do anything? Do you have a bad time for you to do anything? For example you are not a morning person, so you would not like to be disturbed in the morning time?

_____

113. Have you recovered from the pains of past relationships, health, or wealth?

_____

114. Do you believe in the power of a discussion?

_____

115. Are you open to sharing without fear of rejection?

_____

116. Do you believe in sharing chores, money, heartaches, concerns, fun times, intimacy? If not, why?

_____

117. Would you like to change anything in your life today?

_____

118. Would this change be beneficial to your new blended family?

_____

119. Can you think of a question or statement that you believe your chosen mate would benefit by providing an answer to you? If so, write it down then share it.

_____

120. Do you love your new chosen mate and your destiny of happiness enough to share your responses in a controlled environment and agree that the discussions are just the beginning bridge to bring your love closer and closer and closer?

_____

End Notes:

We recommend that you both focus on the relationship between you and your new chosen mate. Allow your love to transform you, your chosen mate and children into a new blended family by changing the way you think, react, speak and feel. It is at this point you both will agree that you are *a lethal weapon* that is armed with your love for each other, your unified goals for your blended family and being successful at *taking the step out of step parenting*. These are the only winning options.

Tips for your successful journey

- ❖ Keep your eyes on the goal and remember sometimes the trips will be tough.
- ❖ You will be traveling charted but not navigated waters that will require energy, time, patience, understanding and honesty. All of these can be demanding!
- ❖ Don't give up. Keep your eyes on the goal; the end results will be treasured.
- ❖ Remember the rule: never hike or hunt alone - Take this journey together.
- ❖ Remember to encourage and not discourage along the way
- ❖ Remember to try to help and not try to hurt
- ❖ Remember to stand together because division is a major cause of Falling and Failing
- ❖ Celebrate the bridge crossing of each roadblock, troubled waters or stumbling block.

www.ingramcontent.com/pod-product-compliance
Lightning Source LLC
Chambersburg PA
CBHW081149090426
42736CB00017B/3251